United States Department of Agriculture

Forest Service

Rocky Mountain Research Station

Resource Bulletin RMRS-RB-12

January 2012

Idaho's Forest Products Industry and Timber Harvest, 2006

Jason P. Brandt, Todd A. Morgan, Charles E. Keegan, III, Jon M. Songster, Timothy P. Spoelma, Larry T. DeBlander

I0435130

Abstract

This report traces the flow of Idaho's 2006 timber harvest through the primary wood-using industries; describes the structure, capacity, and condition of Idaho's primary forest products industry; and quantifies volumes and uses of wood fiber. Wood products industry historical trends and changes in harvest, production, employment, and sales are also examined.

Keywords: forest economics, mill residue, timber processors, wood utilization

Authors

Jason P. Brandt is a contract specialist with the National Interagency Fire Center, Boise, Idaho.

Todd A. Morgan is the Director of Forest Industry Research, and Charles E. Keegan is a Research Associate at the Bureau of Business and Economic Research, Gallagher Business Building, The University of Montana, Missoula, Montana.

Jon M. Songster is a Program Assistant with U.S. Department of Agriculture, Natural Resource Conservation Service, Coudersport, Pennsylvania.

Timothy P. Spoelma is a Silviculturist with the Montana Department of Natural Resources, Forest Management Bureau, Missoula, Montana.

Larry T. DeBlander is a Forester, U.S. Department of Agriculture, Forest Service, Rocky Mountain Research Station, Forestry Sciences Laboratory, Ogden, Utah.

Highlights

- A total of 97 timber-processing facilities were identified as active in Idaho during 2006:
    - 35 Sawmills
    - 3 Plywood / veneer plants
    - 24 Log home facilities
    - 12 Residue related products facilities
    - 7 Cedar product mills
    - 16 Post, pole, and log furniture manufacturers

- Idaho's total timber harvest in 2006 was just under 1,121 million board feet (MMBF) Scribner, approximately 11 percent higher than the timber harvest in 2001.

- Saw and veneer logs made up over 91 percent of the total harvest. Clearwater, Shoshone, and Benewah counties were the largest contributors to the state's total harvest in 2006.

- Idaho was a net importer of nearly 30 MMBF Scribner of timber in 2006. About 89 MMBF of timber harvested in Idaho was shipped outside of the state for processing, and nearly 119 MMBF of timber harvested in other states was processed in Idaho.

- Idaho sawmills recovered 1.89 board feet lumber tally per board foot Scribner of log input, about a 2 percent increase in recovery from 2001.

- The number of Idaho sawmills has declined by 76 percent since 1979, while total capacity has fallen 37 percent to 1,304 MMBF Scribner of timber annually.

- Idaho mills with annual capacity of more than 50 MMBF accounted for over 80 percent of Idaho's sawtimber processing capacity in 2006 compared to 61 percent in 2001 and just 39 percent in 1995.

- Timber harvested in Idaho is being transported greater distances to primary processors in the state. Since 1985, the portion of timber received by primary processors that was harvested in the county where it was processed declined by 18 percent as receipts from other counties increased by 13 percent.

- Idaho's primary forest products industry shipped products valued at $1.6 billion (f.o.b. the producing mill) in 2006. Lumber and plywood/veneer contributed 48 percent of total sales while residue related products such as pulp and paper, and particleboard represented 47 percent.

- Idaho's 35 sawmills produced over 1.8 billion feet of lumber, which when combined with the plywood and veneer facilities generated over 1.5 million bone-dry units of wood residue.

Contents

Introduction

The purpose of this report is to describe the utilization of Idaho's 2006 timber harvest and the conditions, structure, and operations of the state's primary forest products industry. Primary forest products manufacturers are firms that process timber into manufactured products such as lumber, and facilities such as pulp and paper mills and particleboard plants that use the wood fiber residue directly from timber processors. This report also describes recent and historical trends in use of the state's timber resources including raw material sources, inventory, growth, and harvest. Other topics covered in the report include the extent and efficiency of Idaho's processing infrastructure and the volume and value of finished products and residues.

Information in this report is primarily generated through a periodic, statewide census of manufacturers of primary forest products. The census also includes firms in adjacent states that utilized timber harvested in Idaho during the 2006 calendar year. This census is conducted by the University of Montana's Bureau of Business and Economic Research (BBER) in cooperation with the USDA Forest Service, Interior West Forest Inventory and Analysis (IW-FIA) program.

Forest Industries Data Collection System

The Forest Industries Data Collection System (FIDACS) was developed by the BBER in cooperation with the FIA programs in the Rocky Mountain and Pacific Northwest Research Stations to collect, compile, and report data from primary forest products manufacturers.

Primary forest products firms were identified through the use of various directories, industry associations, internet searches, and through previous censuses. Questionnaires are distributed by mail, fax, or email and are administered over the telephone when necessary. A single questionnaire is completed for each processing facility, and includes the following information:

- Plant production, capacity, and employment
- Volume of raw material received, by county and ownership
- Species mix and proportion of standing dead timber received
- Finished product volumes, types, sales value, and market locations
- Utilization and marketing of manufacturing residue

Similar censuses have been conducted periodically in the Pacific Coast and Rocky Mountain States for over 30 years by the BBER and Forest Service research stations. Previous FIDACS censuses were completed for Idaho in 1979, 1980, 1985, 1990, 1995, and 2001 (Godfrey and others 1980; Keegan and others 1982, 1988, 1992, 1997; Morgan and others 2004). Information collected through FIDACS is stored at the University of Montana's BBER. Additional information is available by request; however, individual firm-level data are confidential and will not be released.

The Operating Environment of Idaho's Forest Products Industry

Since the late 1970s, the forest products industry has been characterized by extreme changes in markets and operating conditions. Driven by a strong U.S. economy that included annual housing starts averaging 1.8 million units (fig. 1),

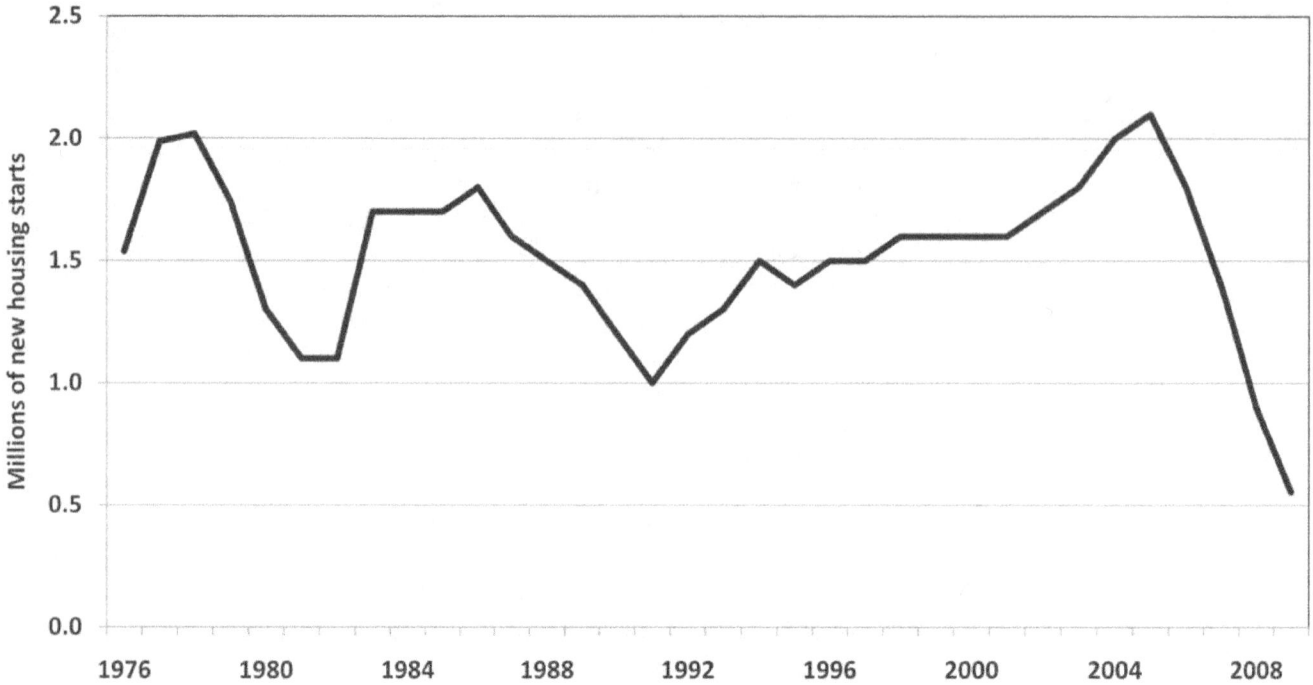

Figure 1—United States housing starts 1976 through 2009 (source: U.S. Census Bureau 2009).

the late 1970s was a period of high prices for wood products (WWPA 1964-2010), as well as a period of relatively abundant timber in Idaho. A recession began in the last quarter of 1979, and the first few years of the 1980s saw the most difficult operating conditions since the Great Depression. Official recessions occurred periodically between 1980 and 1982, with low levels of construction activity, particularly in 1982. From 1983 to 1985, there were near record levels of forest products consumption in the United States but low prices for lumber (Random Lengths 1976-2009).The low prices were due primarily to the high value of the U.S. dollar, leading to declines in export and increases in imports, channeling large volumes of foreign wood and paper products into U.S. markets.

Not until the last half of the 1980s did markets begin to improve, with prices of wood products increasing due to a strong economy and lower U.S. dollar. Because of low timber harvest during the early 1980s, Idaho timber processors had substantial volume under contract that yielded a temporary abundance of timber in the late 1980s; harvest and output reached record or near record levels.

Restricted timber availability throughout the western United States and global market conditions both have had major impacts on the forest products industry since the early 1990s. Declines in harvests from Federal timberland (primarily National Forests) in the western United States led to capacity losses throughout the west and spurred expansion in other regions. Most pertinent to U.S. markets were expansions in eastern Canada and the southeastern United States.

The decline in timber harvests on National Forests across the West and in Idaho during the 1990s resulted from numerous constraints on harvesting timber on Federal lands, including threatened and endangered species protection, appeals and litigation of timber sales, and cumulative impacts of past harvesting on resources such as wildlife, aesthetics, and fisheries (Haminishi and others 1995). Harvest from Federal timberlands in the western United States fell by approximately 8 billion board feet, a decline of about 80 percent. This volume is equivalent to about

14 percent of the U.S. harvest of softwood timber. Idaho's National Forest timber harvest volume fell sharply following 1990. The 2004-2006 average timber harvest was only 16 percent of the 1990 level, with the total harvest across all ownerships falling 35 percent since 1990.

Global economic conditions were also important to the forest products industry in the 1990s. A recession occurred after the first Gulf War due to a variety of factors, which led to low lumber prices. However, in 1993 and much of 1994, the market swung to the other extreme. Lumber prices rose to near record levels due to high demand, driven by strengthening U.S. and global economies and significant reductions in the Federal timber supply. Markets weakened modestly in 1995, stemming from slowing U.S. and international economies. Additionally, rising imports of Canadian lumber became an increasingly contentious issue as consumption slackened in 1995 and the Canadian dollar weakened. In 1996, the United States and Canadian governments agreed to a 5-year quota on Canadian timber-producing provinces. This led to strong lumber prices until mid-1997, when a severe economic decline in Japan and other Asian countries weakened the demand for wood products.

In 1999, markets improved considerably due to the U.S. economy's strong performance and some improvements in the global economy. However, the situation changed dramatically again in 2000, as a drop in housing starts in the United States and Japan, and a strong U.S. dollar led to low softwood lumber prices. With a U.S. recession in 2001 (exacerbated by the September 11 World Trade Center terrorist attacks), the renegotiation of the U.S.-Canada Softwood Lumber Agreement, and a continuously strengthening dollar, prices for lumber and other wood and paper products dropped to their lowest levels since the 1991 recession.

Low lumber prices persisted despite low interest rates and record high U.S. lumber consumption, topping 56 billion board feet in 2002 (Random Lengths 1976-2009; WWPA 1964-2010). Prices for lumber and panel products rebounded in late 2003 when U.S. housing starts surged as a result of relaxed lending practices, declining interest rates, and the weakened value of the dollar (fig. 1). Prices for lumber continued to rise during 2004 and 2005.U.S. housing starts exceeded two million, demand for wood products was strong, and prices reached their highest level since the late 1990s. Strong global markets and hurricanes in the southeastern United States brought on additional demand for wood products. During 2006, a decline in the U.S. housing market led to sharp decreases in prices for most wood products. High fuel costs during the summer months also led to higher logging and transportation costs.

Since 2006, conditions for Idaho's forest industry have deteriorated further (Morgan and others 2011). Timber harvest and lumber production volumes have dropped by more than 25 percent and 35 percent, respectively. Through 2009, domestic lumber consumption and new housing starts remained at recessionary lows, prices for finished lumber dropped more than 30 percent, and total wood products sales from Idaho's forest industry declined by more than 25 percent (Brandt and others 2010; WWPA 2010). In 2010, lumber consumption in the United States remained at historically low levels; however, softwood lumber exports increased by more than 50 percent. Annual U.S. housing starts fell to 554,000 units during 2009—their lowest level in more than six decades—but were up slightly to just under 590,000 units for 2010. Despite the low level of housing starts, there was a jump in lumber prices in 2010. In response to curtailed production at mills throughout North America, rising exports, and a slight uptick in housing starts, lumber prices were approximately 27 percent higher than the very low levels experienced

USDA Forest Service Resour. Bull. RMRS-RB-12. 2012

3

in 2009. Expectations are for gradual improvement in markets through 2011 and 2012 with substantial improvements after 2012 as U.S. home building recovers and global demand continues to increase. This should lead to a substantial rise in the output of Idaho's wood and paper products industry.

Idaho's 2006 Timber Harvest, Products, and Flow

Idaho Timberlands

About 40 percent of the total land area in Idaho is covered by 21.4 million acres of forest. Almost 3.6 million acres of Idaho forest lands are reserved through statute or administrative designation, such as National Forest Wilderness areas and National Parks and Monuments, and not available for timber production. The remaining 17.8 million acres are non-reserved forest land, of which 16.6 million acres is considered non-reserved timberland available for timber production. Based on the Idaho 2004-2009 Forest Inventory and Analysis (FIA) data, the USDA Forest Service's National Forest System manages nearly 74 percent of the state's non-reserved timberlands (table 1). However, more than 8 million acres are National Forest roadless areas that are unlikely to be developed for timber production. The remaining non-reserved timberlands are divided between nonindustrial private owners including tribal (8.6 percent), Idaho state endowment lands (7.1 percent), industrial private lands (6.8 percent), Bureau of Land Management (3.7 percent), and other public ownership (0.1 percent).

Ownership of industrial private timberlands in Idaho has undergone major changes since 2001. Many large forest products companies that once sought a high level of vertical integration to reduce operating costs have reorganized their timberlands into real estate investment trusts (REITs) or sold them to timberland investment management organizations (TIMOs), which now control over 1 million acres of land in Idaho. In addition to managing forests for the sale of timber, REITs and TIMOs evaluate land parcels for their real estate potential on the open market and generate revenue through the sale of recreation permits to allow access to timberlands.

Table 1—Idaho non-reserved timberland by ownership class.

Ownership class	Acres -(2004-2009)	Percentage of non-reserved timberland
National Forest	12,226,687	73.6
Undifferentiated private	2,571,621	15.5
State	1,183,182	7.1
Bureau of Land Management	613,787	3.7
Other public	21,543	0.1
All owners	16,616,821	100.0

Harvest Trends 1947 through 2006

The USDA Forest Service has kept comprehensive annual harvest data by ownership in Idaho since 1969. Other sources of information were used to develop harvest numbers for 1947 through 1969 (fig. 2). While detailed harvest by ownership could not be developed for all years, the harvest estimates are reasonable representations of total harvest and harvest trends. Total harvest and non-National Forest harvest were estimated for 1947 through 1958; harvest data for private land, National Forests, and other public land have been produced for subsequent years. Idaho's timber harvest climbed from about 1,150 MMBF Scribner in 1947 to about 1,800 MMBF in the late 1960s. The major factor change in harvest during this period was the increase in National Forest harvest, from 250 MMBF in 1947 to an all time high of more than 1 billion board feet annually in 1968, 1969, and 1976. Post World War II public policy encouraged increased harvest on Federal lands to meet the strong national demand for building materials. As a result, the share of Idaho's harvest from the National Forests increased from less than 30 percent in the 1940s to 60 percent in the late 1960s.

Timber harvest levels increased further in the 1970s, and the peak harvest for Idaho occurred in 1976 at 1.9 billion board feet Scribner. National Forest harvest in the late 1970s was slightly below the late 1960s; the increase in total harvest came primarily from private timberlands. In the late 1970s, National Forests provided about half of Idaho's timber harvest. Private lands provided about 40 percent of the

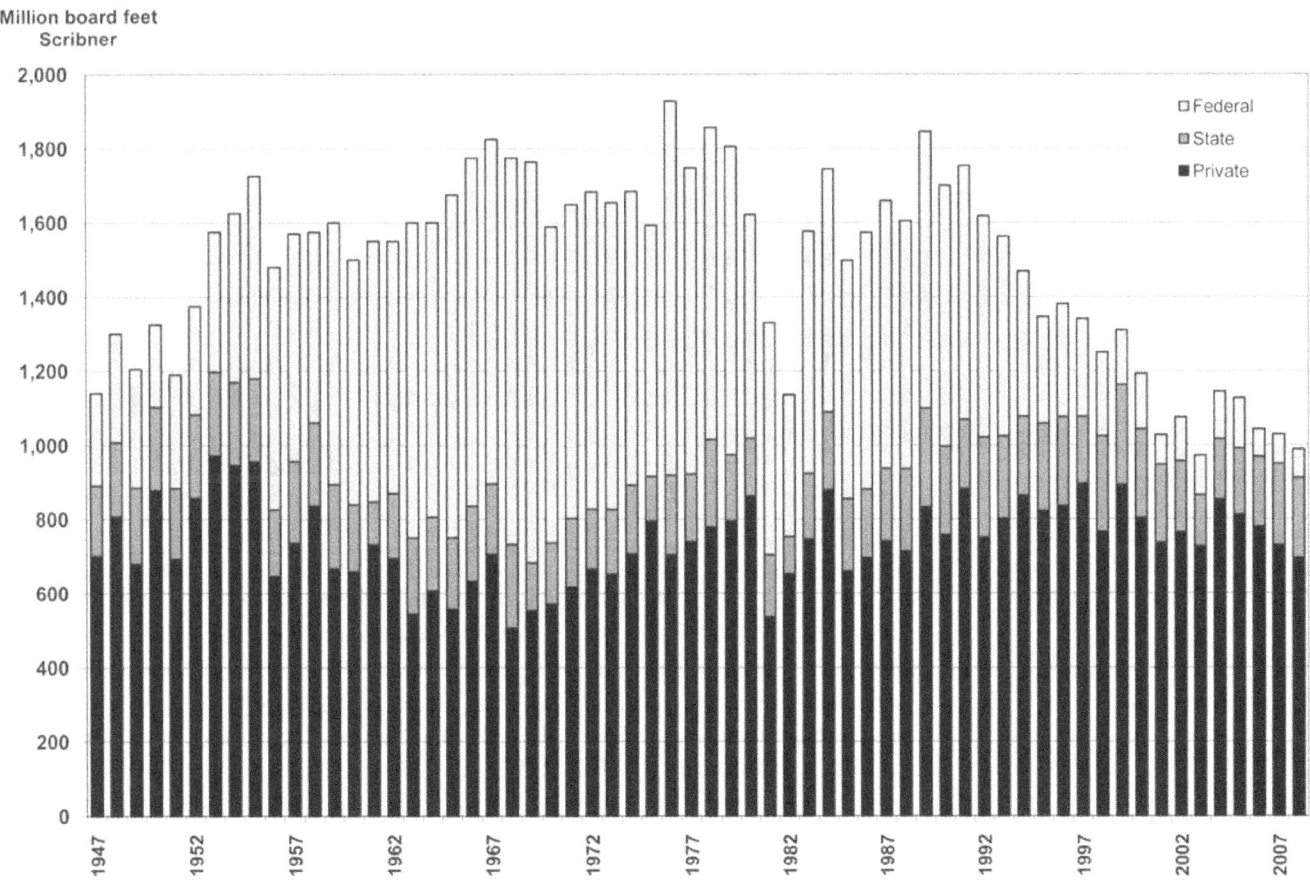

Figure 2—Idaho's timber harvest by ownership, 1947 through 2008 (source: Brandt and others 2009).

harvest in the late 1970s versus 33 percent in the late 1960s. Most of the remaining harvest in the 1970s was from Idaho State lands. During the recession years of the early 1980s, harvest fell sharply, but rebounded in the last half of the 1980s to an average level of 1,635 MMBF. By the late 1980s, harvest from National Forest lands had slipped to 45 percent, and harvest from private lands increased to about 45 percent. Harvest from Idaho Department of Lands and Bureau of Land Management forest lands made up the remaining 10 percent.

Throughout the 1990s and into the 2000s, Idaho's total timber harvest declined steadily because of a dramatic decline in harvest from National Forest lands. In 2001, the National Forest harvest for Idaho was the lowest since WWII and only 11 percent of what it was in 1990. The National Forest harvest declined by 629 MMBF from 1990 to 2001 and during that time accounted for 94 percent of Idaho's total harvest decline (673 MMBF). The volume of timber harvested from Idaho's private timberlands remained stable throughout the 1990s and into the new century; however, the proportion of the harvest coming from private lands increased steadily from 45 percent (732MMBF) in 1990 to 72 percent (750 MMBF) in 2001 and 74 percent (834 MMBF) in 2006. Harvest from Idaho's other public lands has followed a similar trend, with harvest volumes remaining fairly stable, but the proportion of the total harvest increasing from 14 percent (259 MMBF) in 1990 to 21 percent (179 MMBF) in 2001 and 19 percent (208 MMBF) in 2006. In 1998, the harvest volume from other public lands in Idaho surpassed the volume harvested from Idaho's National Forests for the first time on record. Timber harvested from state lands accounted for approximately 18 percent (201 MMBF) of Idaho's total harvest in 2006 and about 97 percent of harvest from "other public" lands. Harvest from Bureau of Land Management (BLM) lands remained a small fraction of harvest from "other public" lands in 2006.

Harvest by Geographic Source

Counties north of the Salmon River supplied 87 percent of the 2006 timber harvest and 13 percent came from counties south of the Salmon River (table 2). During 2006, Shoshone County's harvest exceeded the Clearwater County harvest and led the state at 200 MMBF—about 18 percent of total harvest. Other leading timber-producing counties were Clearwater with 174 MMBF; Benewah with 144 MMBF; Latah with 125 MMBF; Kootenai with 100 MMBF; and Bonner with 93 MMBF. Together, these six counties in northern Idaho supplied 75 percent of Idaho's timber harvest.

Valley County had the largest harvest in southern Idaho at 65 MMBF, which was 6 percent of the state's harvest. Valley, Adams, and Boise counties contributed a combined 11 percent of the state's harvest. Harvest volumes in 2006 for both northern and southern Idaho were higher than the 2001 census but lower than the 1995 census. Since 1979, the harvest has declined by 434 MMBF (31 percent) in northern Idaho and 295 MMBF (67 percent) in southern Idaho. Compared to 2001, the harvest was up 8 percent in northern Idaho and 8 percent in southern Idaho.

Northern Idaho's most dramatic county-level changes from 1979 to 2006 occurred in Clearwater and Idaho counties where the combined harvest dropped by 495 MMBF (67 percent)—370 MMBF in Clearwater county and 125 MMBF in Idaho County. From 1979 to 1990, the harvest in Clearwater county fell by 182 MMBF (56 percent) from private lands and 89 MMBF (66 percent) drop in the National Forest harvest. Since 1990, Clearwater County's harvest has declined on National Forest lands by 84 percent, 48 percent decline on state lands, and

Table 2—Idaho timber harvest (MMBF, Scribner) by county, selected years (sources: Keegan and others 1982,1988,1992,1997; Morgan and others 2004).

County	1979 MMBF Scribner	1979 Percent of total	1985 MMBF Scribner	1985 Percent of total	1990 MMBF Scribner	1990 Percent of total	1995 MMBF Scribner	1995 Percent of total	2001 MMBF Scribner	2001 Percent of total	2006 MMBF Scribner	2006 Percent of Total
Northern Idaho												
Clearwater	544	29.0	335	21.0	267	16.0	234	17.0	182	18.0	174	15.6
Shoshone	206	11.0	217	14.0	183	11.0	194	14.0	172	17.0	200	17.8
Idaho	190	10.0	156	10.0	174	10.0	113	8.0	65	6.0	65	5.8
Bonner	142	8.0	175	11.0	197	12.0	139	10.0	124	12.0	93	8.3
Benewah	100	5.0	94	6.0	152	9.0	117	9.0	129	13.0	144	12.9
Boundary	94	5.0	80	5.0	86	5.0	69	5.0	57	6.0	53	4.8
Kootenai	65	4.0	80	5.0	152	9.0	114	8.0	81	8.0	100	8.9
Latah	57	3.0	89	6.0	84	5.0	96	7.0	70	7.0	125	11.2
Nez Perce	8	0.0	12	1.0	17	1.0	8	1.0	4	0.0	10	0.9
Lewis	4	0.0	13	1.0	20	1.0	17	1.0	14	1.0	12	1.1
Northern Idaho	**1,410**	**76.0**	**1,254**	**79.0**	**1,332**	**79.0**	**1,100**	**80.0**	**899**	**89.0**	**976**	**87.1**
Southern Idaho												
Valley	107	6.0	88	6.0	52	3.0	67	5.0	39	4.0	65	5.8
Boise	84	4.0	67	4.0	127	8.0	93	7.0	20	2.0	25	2.2
Adams	52	3.0	66	4.0	87	5.0	28	2.0	25	2.0	30	2.7
Washington	4	b	9	1.0	4	b	6	b	-	b	c	b
Elmore	25	1.0	14	1.0	5	b	38	3.0	7	1.0	c	b
Other counties	20	1.0	3	b	6	b	11	1.0	1	b	6	0.5
Southwestern Idaho	**292**	**16.0**	**247**	**16.0**	**281**	**17.0**	**242**	**18.0**	**91**	**9.0**	**126**	**11.3**
Fremont	76	4.0	43	3.0	20	1.0	2	b	3	b	1	0.1
Lemhi	34	2.0	11	1.0	16	1.0	6	b	1	b	1	0.1
Clark	10	1.0	10	1.0	16	1.0	-	b	1	b	6	0.6
Caribou	4	b	10	1.0	3	b	5	b	5	b	4	0.3
Other counties	24	1.0	19	1.0	24	1.0	15	1.0	7	1.0	7	0.6
Southeastern Idaho	**148**	**8.0**	**93**	**6.0**	**79**	**5.0**	**27**	**2.0**	**17**	**2.0**	**19**	**1.7**
Southern Idaho	**440**	**24.0**	**340**	**21.0**	**360**	**21.0**	**269**	**20.0**	**108**	**11.0**	**145**	**12.9**
Idaho Total	**1850**	**100.0**	**1594**	**100.0**	**1692**	**100.0**	**1,370**	**100.0**	**1,007**	**100.0**	**1,121**	**100.0**

[a] Percentage detail may not sum to 100% due to rounding.

[b] Less than 0.05 percent.

[c] Less than 1 MMBF

USDA Forest Service Resour. Bull. RMRS-RB-12. 2012

7

4 percent on industrial lands. In Idaho County, the harvest from National Forest lands fell 90 percent since 1990 and by 30 percent from other ownerships during that time.

Southern Idaho's most dramatic harvest decreases occurred in the southwestern counties of Adams, Boise, and Valley, where timber harvest has decreased by 146 MMBF since 1990 (table 2). Virtually all of these reductions can be attributed to sharply declining harvest levels from National Forest lands, which dropped by approximately 87 percent since 1990. The harvest from other ownerships has remained essentially unchanged over the same period.

Harvest by Ownership and Product Type

Total timber harvest in Idaho increased by approximately 10 percent to 1.121 billion board feet Scribner from 2001 to 2006. Harvest increased across all ownerships except on tribal lands. Harvest on public lands increased by 11 percent in 2006 compared to 2001. Harvest in Idaho from public lands has drastically declined since 1990 (table 3).

About 91 percent of Idaho's harvest is processed into lumber and plywood. Private lands continue to be the primary source of saw and veneer logs, providing 76 percent (776 MMBF) of the total supply in 2006 (table 4). Private lands accounted for about 76 percent (726 MMBF) in 2001 and 59 percent (711 MMBF) in 1995. Prior to 1995, private lands provided less than half of Idaho's saw and veneer log harvest (Keegan and others 1997; Morgan and others 2004). During 2006, National Forests provided just 6 percent (63 MMBF) of Idaho's saw and veneer log harvest, compared to 7 percent (71 MMBF) in 2001, 23 percent (272 MMBF) in 1995, and over 40 percent prior to 1995.

Idaho's pulpwood harvest increased from 3.4 MMBF in 2001 to 51.3 MMBF in 2006. Strong pulpwood markets often occur at infrequent and unpredictable intervals, usually when lumber production is down and paper markets are strong. Idaho's major industrial timberland owner has been reorganized as a REIT, and a spin-off firm operates the only pulp and paper mill in the state; presumably the two firms are in a mutually advantageous position to recognize and immediately respond to pulpwood market opportunities. The pulp and paper sector typically relies on private lands for a large portion of their roundwood receipts. Private

Table 3—Proportion of Idaho timber harvest (MBF, Scribner) by ownership class, selected years (sources: Keegan and others 1982,1988,1992,1997; Morgan and others 2004).

Ownership class	1979	1985	1990	1995	2001	2006
	- - - - - - Thousand board feet, Scribner - - - - - -					
Private	808,749	779,109	754,978	829,417	750,357	833,797
Industrial	455,721	467,474	364,178	467,518	443,029	485,590
Non-industrial private	353,028	311	390,800	361,899	295,704	343,237
Tribal	[a]	[a]	[a]	[a]	11,857	4,970
Public	1,041,719	814,787	937,560	540,296	256,704	286,813
National Forest	866,455	631,003	700,715	301,277	77,863	78,613
Other public[b]	175,264	183,784	236,845	239,019	178,841	208,200
All owners[b]	1,850,468	1,593,896	1,692,538	1,369,713	1,007,061	1,120,610

[a]Tribal harvest included in non-industrial private
[b]Other public refers to state owned timberlands and Bureau of Land Management timberlands

Table 4—Idaho timber harvest by ownership class and timber product 2006.

Ownership class	Saw and veneer logs[b]	House logs	Cedar products	Other timber products[a]	All products
- *Thousand board feet, Scribner* -					
Private timberlands	775,929	832	12,909	44,127	833,797
Industrial	441,501	60	9,289	34,740	485,590
Non-industrial private	330,378	772	3,620	8,467	343,237
Tr bal	4,050	-	-	920	4,970
Public timberlands	246,281	13,349	9,710	17,473	286,813
National Forest	62,965	12,439	500	2,709	78,613
Other public	183,316	910	9,210	14,764	208,200
All owners	**1,022,210**	**14,181**	**22,619**	**61,600**	**1,120,610**

[a]Other timber products include logs used for pulpwood, posts and poles, firewood, furniture logs, and energywood logs.
[b]Saw and veneer logs combined to prevent disclosure of firm level data.

timberlands supplied 77 percent (41 MMBF) of the pulpwood harvest in 2006, 80 percent (3 MMBF) in 2001, 84 percent (88MMBF) in 1995, and 64 percent (29 MMBF) in 1990. The difference in the private harvest of pulpwood among census years is a reflection of the strength of the pulp market during those years.

In 2006, the harvest for cedar products, house logs, posts, poles, rails, and other products combined totaled 46 MMBF. Harvest of this group of products was 43 MMBF in 2001 and 65 MMBF in 1995. Public timberlands provided 63 percent of the harvest for this group of products in 2006. This is a greater proportion than in 2001 (52 percent) or in 1995 (53 percent). The total harvest of cedar products in 2006 (22.6 MMBF) decreased from the 2001 harvest (29.5 MMBF) while the total harvest for post, poles, and rails increased from 7.3 MMBF in 2001 to 8.4 MMBF in 2006. Public land provided 43 percent of the harvest for cedar products and 59 percent of the harvest for posts, poles, and rails. The largest increase among these products was for the purpose of house log products. Harvest of material for house logs more than doubled during this time from 6.5 MMBF in 2001 to over 14 MMBF in 2006. National Forests continued to supply the majority of house logs, increasing from 82 percent in 2001 to nearly 88 percent in 2006.

Harvest by Species

True firs (*Abies* spp.)—grand fir (Abies grandis (Doug. Ex D. Don) Lindl.) and subalpine fir (Abies lasiocarpa (Hook.) Nutt.)—represented the largest species component of Idaho's 2006 timber harvest at 34 percent (table 5). Douglas-fir (*Pseudotsuga menziesii* (Mirb.) Franco) was the second largest species component of the 2006 harvest, despite a 2 percent proportional increase in the Douglas-fir harvest from the 2001 census. The increases in proportion of both species groups offset losses of western hemlock (*Tsuga heterophylla* (Raf.) Sarg.) and western larch (*Larix occidentalis* Nutt.) harvest reductions in 2006. The decline in western white pine (*Pinus monticola* Dougl. ex D. Don) harvest has been the greatest change in harvested timber species composition in Idaho over the last 30 years. The white pine harvest was about 343 MMBF and accounted for 19 percent of Idaho's timber harvest in 1969; by 2001 the white pine timber harvest had dropped to just 4 percent or 39 MMBF. By 2006 western white pine harvest had further

USDA Forest Service Resour. Bull. RMRS-RB-12. 2012

9

Table 5—Proportion of Idaho timber harvest by species, selected years (sources: Setzer and Wilson 1970; Morgan and others 2004).

Species	1969	1979	1985	1990	1995	2001	2006
				Percentage of harvest (MBF, Scribner)			
True firs	24	22	27	23	25	24	34
Douglas-fir	18	20	21	22	27	26	28
Western hemlock	b	1	3	3	4	12	4
Western redcedar	7	11	10	11	9	10	13
Western larch	6	6	6	6	6	10	5
Ponderosa pine	14	13	12	18	17	7	7
Lodgepole pine	4	8	10	10	6	5	5
Western white pine	19	8	6	5	3	4	1
Spruces	a	3	5	3	2	2	2
Other species[a]	8	9	1	0	2	0	1
All species[b]	100	100	100	100	100	100	100

[a]Western hemlock and Englemann spruce were included in the other species group in 1969.
[b]Percentage detail may not sum to 100%.

declined to just 1 percent of the total. This change is the result of several interacting factors including mortality caused by white pine blister rust and bark beetles, high-grade logging, and changes in forest species composition related, in part, to fire suppression. By far the biggest blow to white pine has been dealt by white pine blister rust, an exotic disease introduced to the United States from Europe in the early 1900s. Blister rust had reached epidemic levels in the 1940s and has significantly damaged the white pine resource throughout the Inland Northwest (Fins and others 2001).

In 2006, all of Idaho's species groups were used to produce lumber. As in 2001, true firs were the species most frequently harvested for saw and veneer logs, comprising 34 percent of the saw and veneer log harvest, while Douglas-fir accounted for 31 percent (table 6). Western redcedar (*Thuja plicata* Donn ex D. Don) and ponderosa pine (*Pinus ponderosa* Dougl. ex Laws.) represented 9 percent and 7 percent of the saw and veneer log harvest in Idaho, respectively. This is a shift from the 2001 census when Douglas-fir, true firs, western hemlock, and western

Table 6—Idaho timber harvest by species and timber product, 2006.

Species	Saw and veneer logs[a]	House logs	Cedar products	Other timber products[b]	All products
			Thousand board feet, Scribner		
True firs	350,044	37	-	28,400	378,481
Douglas-fir	314,879	2,972	-	467	318,318
Cedar	95,148	137	22,619	23,587	141,491
Ponderosa pine	71,389	1,987	-	216	73,592
Larch	59,488	82	-	-	59,570
Lodgepole pine	49,046	3,387	-	5,563	57,996
Western hemlock	44,390	-	-	400	44,790
Spruce	20,941	5,564	-	419	26,924
Western white pine	15,813	8	-	-	15,821
Other softwoods	402	-	-	2,521	2,923
Hardwoods	670	7	-	27	704
All species	1,022,210	14,181	22,619	61,600	1,120,610

[a]Saw and veneer logs combined to prevent disclosure of firm level data.
[b]Other timber products include logs used for pulpwood, posts and poles, firewood, furniture log, and energywood.

larch were the four most harvested species. This change in the saw log species mix parallels species trends of the 1995, 1990, and 1979 censuses.

Changes in products harvested other than saw and veneer logs can be attributed to the influence of the pulpwood market, which was stronger in 2006 than in 2001, but weaker than in 1995. The 2006 (62 MMBF) harvest of other timber products, including pulpwood, posts and poles, furniture log, energy wood, and noncommercial firewood, was primarily made up of true firs (46 percent), western red cedar (38 percent), and lodgepole pine (*Pinus contorta* Dougl. Ex Loud.) (9 percent). In 2001, Idaho's pulpwood harvest was just 3 MMBF; true firs accounted for 73 percent of this, followed by Douglas-fir (11 percent), and western larch (11 percent). Cedar products harvest was 23 MMBF in 2006, a slight decrease from 2001 (29 MMBF). Similar to 2001, spruce, mostly Engelmann spruce (*Picea engelmannii* Parry ex Engelm.) (39 percent), lodgepole pine (24 percent), and Douglas-fir (21 percent) were the most common species harvested for house logs, though the proportion of lodgepole pine was greater than Douglas-fir in 2006. The primary species harvested for post and pole products were western redcedar (61 percent) and lodgepole pine (36 percent).

Movement of Timber Products

The concentration of production at fewer and larger facilities has created manufacturing centers that draw timber from large geographic areas. Thus, large volumes of timber cross county and state lines. Because many counties, especially in southern Idaho, now have only one or two timber processing facilities, timber movement is described by three broad geographic regions—northern Idaho, southwestern Idaho, and southeastern Idaho—to avoid disclosure of firm-level information concerning timber receipts.

Movement across state lines—In 2006, 8 percent of Idaho's harvest (89 MMBF) was shipped for processing outside of the state (table 7). Idaho's primary wood products manufacturers received 119 MMBF of timber that was harvested outside of Idaho, making the state a net importer of nearly 30 MMBF of timber in 2006. Idaho imported about 32 MMBF in 2001. Previously, Idaho had net exports ranging from 7 to 39 MMBF. None of the timber harvested in Idaho during 2006 was shipped to other countries for processing. Idaho mills did receive over 9 MMBF of timber from Canada in 2006, compared to 28 MMBF in 2001. In 2006, 72 percent (85 MMBF) of Idaho's timber imports came from Washington, 19 percent (22 MMBF) came from Montana, and the balance (3MMBF) came from Wyoming, Utah, Oregon, and Canada.

Table 7—Timber flow into and out of Idaho 2006.

Timber products	Log flow into Idaho	Log flow out of Idaho	Net imports (net exports)
	- - - - - Thousand board feet, Scribner - - - - -		
Saw and veneer logs	110,428	81,682	28,746
House logs	3,045	225	2,820
Cedar products	2,000	1,000	1,000
Other products[a]	3,511	6,536	(3,025)
All products	**118,984**	**89,443**	**29,541**

[a]Other products include logs for pulpwood, posts and poles, log furniture, and industrial fuelwood.

Southern Idaho counties supplied 62 percent (55 MMBF) of Idaho's timber exports to other states in 2006, with southwestern Idaho counties accounting for the majority (46 MMBF) of that volume and northern Idaho counties were the source of the remaining 45 percent (34 MMBF) of timber exports to other states. Saw and veneer logs were the major component of timber harvest flowing into and out of Idaho. In 2006, Idaho sawmills and plywood/veneer mills imported 110 MMBF of saw and veneer logs, while 82 MMBF of saw and veneer logs were exported. Over 3 MMBF of house logs were imported in 2006—2 MMBF for cedar products, along with almost 4 MMBF of logs for other products.

Movement within Idaho—Ninety-two percent (1,031 MMBF) of Idaho's 2006 timber harvest was processed within the state (table 8). Timber movement among Idaho's three regions is somewhat varied. In northern Idaho, 95 percent of timber harvested was processed in the region of harvest. However, in southeastern Idaho, 46 percent of the timber harvested was processed in the region of harvest, and in the southwestern region only 20 percent of timber harvested was processed within the region. Timber movement among counties within the same region showed an increase from 2001 to 2006. Seventy-three percent of the timber harvested in 2006 was processed in a county other than the county of harvest, compared to 68 percent in 2001. These data indicate that timber is traveling a greater distance to be processed and reflects the loss of timber processing capacity in southern Idaho. Since 1985, the portion of timber processed in the county of harvest declined by 18 percent and receipts from other counties increased by 13 percent (fig. 3).

Northern Idaho: The 10 counties north of the Salmon River are the center of Idaho's timber harvesting and processing activities. The total harvest in these counties was about 975 MMBF, or 87 percent of the state's harvest. Ninety-five percent (928 MMBF) of the timber harvested in northern Idaho was processed in northern Idaho, while the remaining 5 percent (48 MMBF) was processed in another region or state. Only 13 MMBF of timber harvest in northern Idaho was processed south of the Salmon River. Thirty percent of timber harvested in northern Idaho was processed in the county of harvest. Fifty-one percent was processed in counties adjacent to (sharing a county line with) the county of harvest, and 15 percent was processed in counties not adjacent to the county of harvest.

Southwestern Idaho: Just over 126 MMBF of timber—11 percent of the state's total harvest—was harvested in the 10 southwestern counties in 2006. Approximately 36 percent (46 MMBF) was processed outside the state. Of the 64 percent (81 MMBF) that was processed in Idaho, 25 MMBF were processed in southwestern Idaho. Thirty-nine percent (49 MMBF) of the southwestern harvest was processed in northern Idaho, with only 5 percent (7 MMBF) processed in southeastern Idaho. Within southwestern Idaho, 8 percent (10 MMBF) of the timber was processed in the county of harvest, while 92 percent (71 MMBF) was processed in other counties. About 51 MMBF (40 percent) was processed in counties adjacent to the county of harvest, and 20 MMBF (15 percent) were processed in counties not adjacent to the county of harvest.

Southeastern Idaho: Southeastern Idaho accounted for the smallest percentage of volume harvested in Idaho in 2006, with 19 MMBF (2 percent). Less than half of this volume (9.2 MMBF) was processed in Idaho; 9.5 MMBF was processed outside the state. Of the 9.2 MMBF processed in Idaho, 93 percent stayed

Table 8—Intra-state and inter-state timber flow of 2006 Idaho timber harvest.

	Intra-state timber flow						Inter-state timber flow		
Region of harvest	Delivered to county of harvest	Delivered to adjacent county	Delivered to non-adjacent county	Total delivered to northern Idaho	Total delivered to southwestern Idaho	Total delivered to southeastern Idaho	Total delivered to Idaho	Total delivered out-of-State	Total harvest
	- - - - - - - - Thousand board feet, Scribner - - - - - - -								
Northern Idaho	290,476	501,013	149,507	927,762	13,234	-	940,996	34,347	975,343
Southwestern Idaho	10,437	50,926	19,572	49,169	25,136	6,630	80,935	45,566	126,501
Southeastern Idaho	2,805	5,825	600	600	-	8,630	9,236	9,530	18,766
Idaho total	303,718	557,764	169,679	977,531	38,370	15,260	1,031,167	89,443	1,120,610
	- - - - - - - Percentage of total harvest - - - - - - -								
Northern Idaho	30	51	15	95	1	-	96	4	87
Southwestern Idaho	8	40	15	39	20	5	64	36	11
Southeastern Idaho	15	31	3	3	-	46	49	51	2
Idaho Total	27	50	15	87	3	1	92	8	100

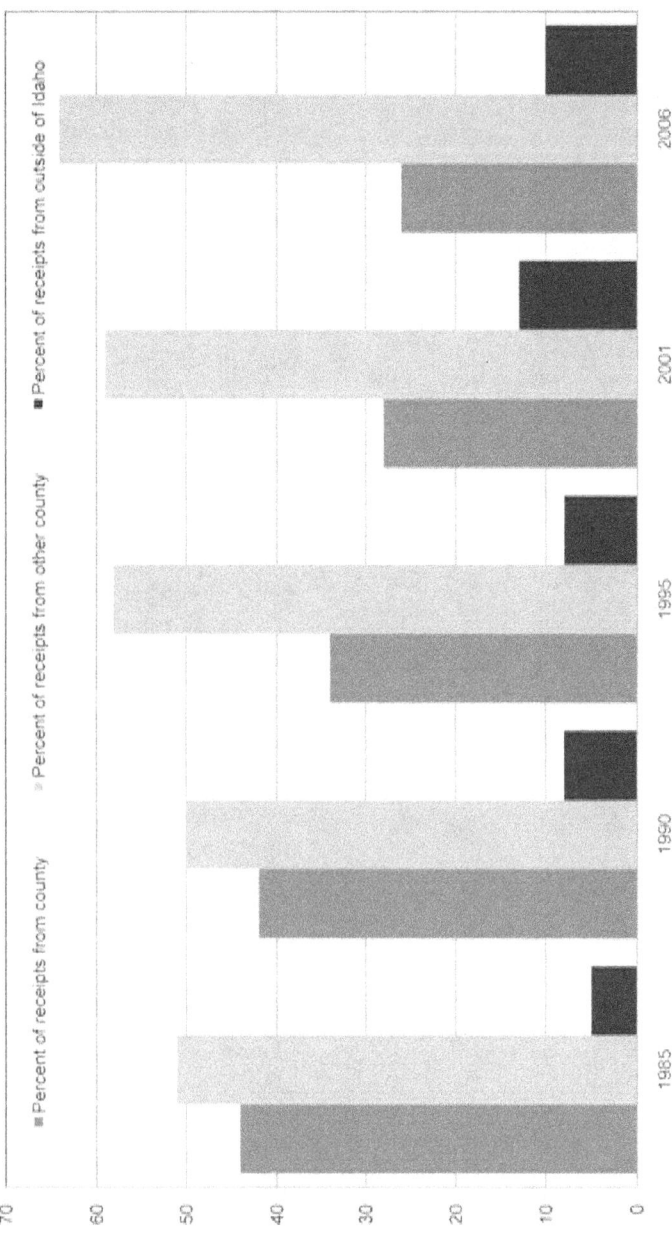

Figure 3—Movement of timber in Idaho.

in southeastern Idaho for processing while the remaining 7 percent was processed in northern Idaho. Of the timber harvested in southeastern Idaho that remained in-state for processing, 63 percent was processed in counties adjacent to the county of harvest, and 30 percent was processed in the county of harvest. The remaining 7 percent was processed in counties not adjacent to the county of harvest.

End Uses of Idaho's Timber

In this section, we trace the flow of Idaho's timber harvest through the state's primary manufacturing sectors. Because both mill residue and products are displayed, volumes are presented in cubic feet rather than board feet Scribner. The following conversion factors were used to convert board foot Scribner volume to cubic foot volume:

- 4.7 board feet per cubic foot for saw and veneer logs
- 5.1 board feet per cubic foot for house logs
- 3.4 board feet per cubic foot for cedar logs
- 3.1 Board feet per cubic foot for post, pole, and log furniture logs
- 2.4 board feet per cubic foot for pulpwood and other timber products

During 2006, Idaho's timber harvest was approximately 259 million cubic feet (MMCF), exclusive of bark (fig. 4). Of this volume, 233 MMCF went to sawmills and plywood plants, 16 MMCF to pulp, 5 MMCF to cedar mills, 3 MMCF to log home manufacturers, and 2 MMCF to posts, poles, and log furniture manufacturers. These figures refer to Idaho's timber harvest and include timber products shipped to out -of-state mills; they do not include timber harvested in other states and processed in Idaho.

Of the 233 MMCF of wood fiber received by sawmills and plywood plants for manufacturing, 120 MMCF (52 percent) became finished lumber, other sawn products, or plywood and veneer products, and 6 MMCF were lost to shrinkage. The remaining 107 MMCF of wood fiber became mill residue. About 93 MMCF of sawmill residue were used as raw material by pulp mills and board plants; 14 MMCF were sold or used internally as hogfuel to generate energy; small volumes of residue were unused.

Pulp and paper mills and other residue using plants, both in Idaho and in other states, received approximately 111 MMCF of wood fiber from Idaho timberlands to be used as raw material for manufacturing products. Only 16 MMCF of that was furnished from timber delivered to pulp and paper mills in round form. Saw and veneer mills supplied 93 MMCF of mill residue to pulp and board manufacturers, and cedar mills and log home manufacturers each added 1 MMCF of residue.

Cedar mills received approximately 5 MMCF of timber, of which 3 MMCF became cedar products. The remaining 2 MMCF were used for hogfuel (1 MMCF), pulp, board, or other residue utilizing plants. Log home manufacturers received 3 MMCF, of which 2 MMCF became house logs, 1 MMCF of residue were utilized by pulp, board, or other residue utilizing plants. Post, pole, and log furniture manufacturers received 2 MMCF of timber with only small volumes utilized for other purposes. Mills in this sector seldom supplied residue for use in other sectors. Most of the residue from this sector was used as firewood, livestock bedding, and mulch.

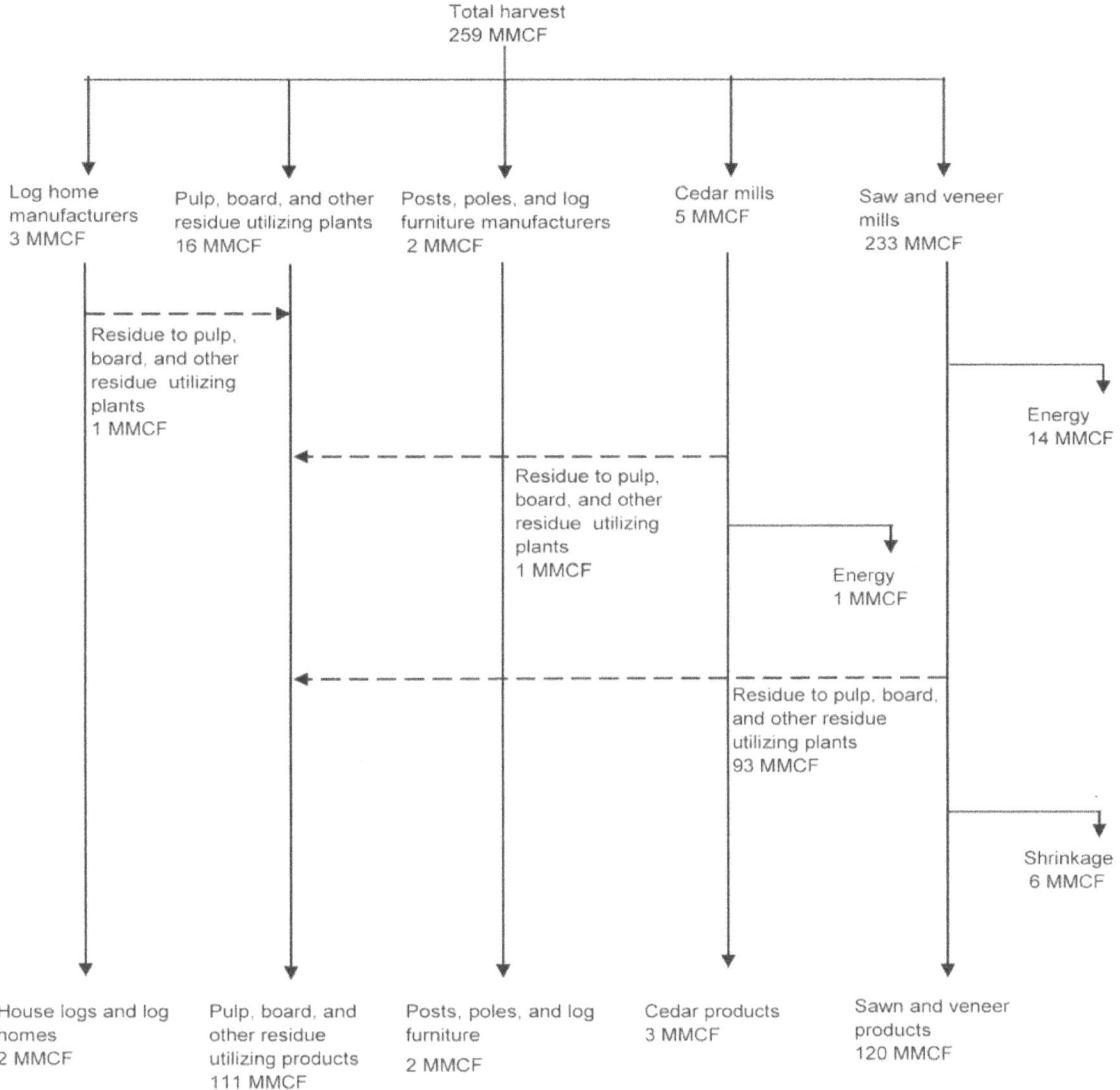

Figure 4—Idaho's timber harvest and flow, 2006.

Structure of Idaho's Forest Products Industry

Structure and Location

In 2006, timber-processing facilities operated in 26 of Idaho's 44 counties, while timber was harvested in 28 counties. Idaho's 10 northern counties contain the greatest concentration of the primary forest products industry (fig. 5), which includes plants that manufacture:

- Lumber and other sawn products
- Veneer/plywood
- Posts, utility poles, small poles, stakes, and roundwood furniture
- House logs and log homes

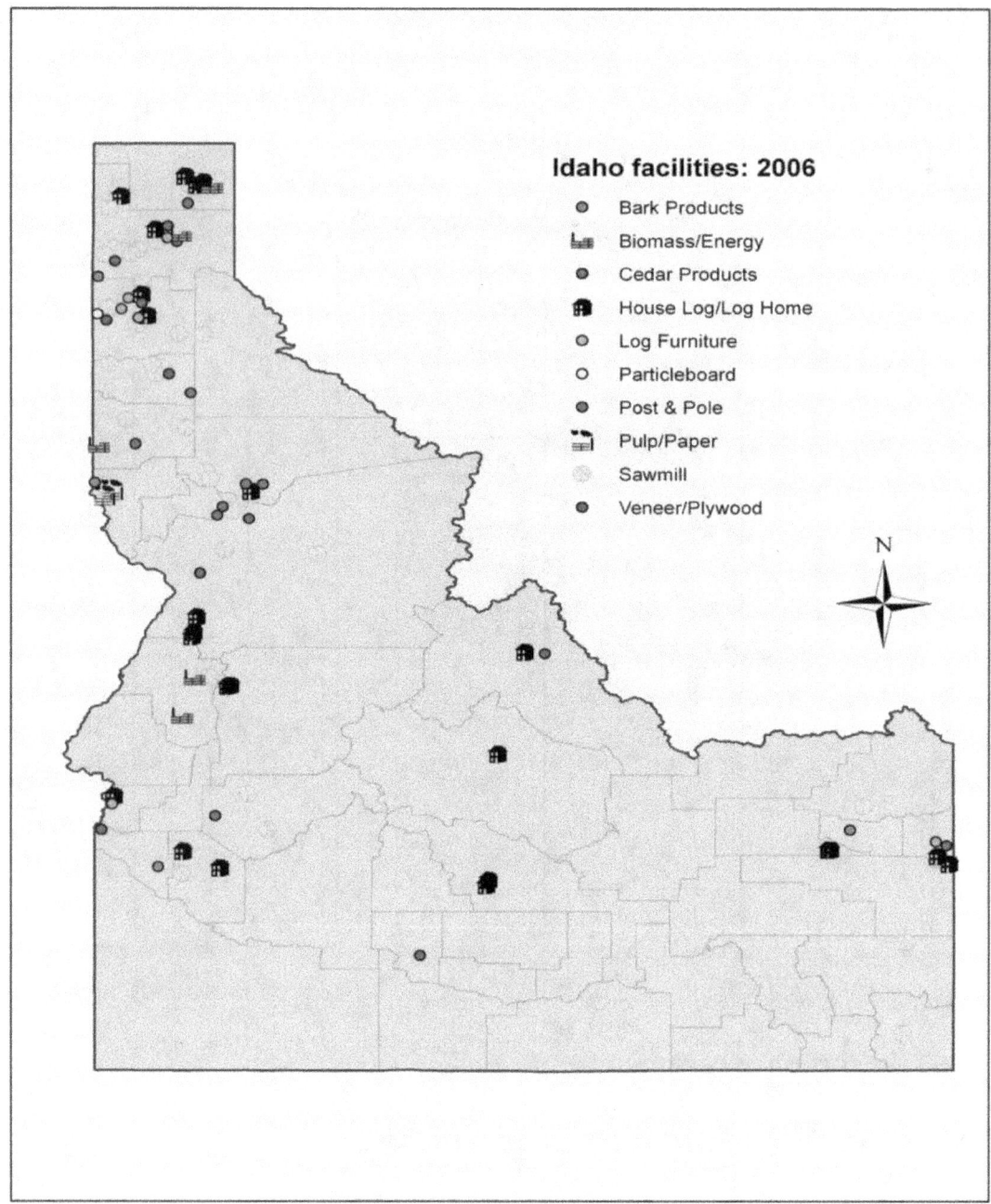

Figure 5—Location of Idaho's active primary forest products manufacturers, 2006.

- Cedar products—shakes, shingles, and split rail fencing
- Other products including pulp and paper, particleboard, chips, decorative bark, wood fuel pellets, and energy from biomass

During 2006, 97 timber-processing facilities operated in Idaho (table 9), 12 fewer than the 2001 census and a decrease of 145 since 1979. The log home sector, which increased by 3 facilities, was the only sector that had growth in the number of facilities since 2001. The number of sawmills in Idaho remained the same while the industry saw losses in all other sectors since 2001. Several large facilities have closed since the last census; these closures are addressed in more detail in the individual sector discussions.

USDA Forest Service Resour. Bull. RMRS-RB-12. 2012

Table 9—Active Idaho primary wood products facilities by county and product during 2006 and other years (sources: Keegan and others 1997; Morgan and others 2004).

County	Lumber	Veneer/plywood	Post, poles, and log furniture	Log homes	Cedar products	Residue-related products[a]	All products
Ada	1			2		1	4
Adams	1					2	3
Bear Lake	1						1
Benewah	4	1			2		7
Blaine				2			2
Boise	2		2				4
Bonner	7	1	3	2		1	14
Boundary	2			3	1	1	7
Canyon			1				1
Car bou	1						1
Clearwater	3			1	1		5
Custer				1			1
Fremont	1						1
Gooding			1				1
Idaho	3		2	4			9
Jefferson				1			1
Kootenai	4	1	4	2		2	13
Latah	2				1	1	4
Lemhi	1		1	1			3
Lewis					2		2
Madison				1		1	2
Nez Perce	1					3	4
Payette			1	1			2
Shoshone	1						1
Teton			1	2			3
Valley				1			1
2006 Total	**35**	**3**	**16**	**24**	**7**	**12**	**97**
2001 Total	35	4	22	21	10	17	109
1995 Total	62	6	32	32	15	15	162
1990 Total	80	6	27	22	26	11	172
1985 Total	90	7	26	20	25	6	174
1979 Total	133	8	35	15	44	7	242

[a]Residue-related products include particleboard, chips, pulp and paper products, bioenergy products, and decorative bark.

Sales Value of Primary Wood Products

Periodic industry censuses (Godfrey and others 1980; Keegan and others 1982,1988,1992,1997; Morgan and others 2004) provide the most complete estimates of sales values for Idaho's primary forest products industry. Various other sources were used to estimate sales values for the non-census years between 1977 and 2007 (Random Lengths 1979-2009; WWPA 1964-2010). All sales are reported free on board (f.o.b.) the producing mill.

Sales by Idaho's primary forest products industry totaled $1.63 billion in 2006 (table 10); estimates for 2007 indicate sales decreased by about $50 million in 2006 dollars and 2008 experienced a much larger decrease of nearly $170 million in 2006 dollars (Brandt and others 2009). Average annual sales for 1977

Table 10—Sales value of Idaho's primary wood products, 1979 through 2006 (sources:Keegan and others 1982,1988,1992,1997; Morgan and others 2004).

Product	1979	1985	1990	1995	2001	2006
			Million 2006 dollars			
Lumber, timbers, other sawn products	1,295.2	727.4	789.6	897.9	771.8	780.9[b]
Residue-related products[a]	624.7	657.2	810.7	866.6	912.1	767.4
Plywood and veneer	219.5	137.6	152.9	216.3	78.5	[b]
House logs and log homes	20.1	5.6	14.8	26.3	28.6	37.9
Cedar products	33.7	13.7	20.5	17.6	34.1	33.5
Posts, poles, and log furniture	42.4	21.4	38.4	32.9	24.9	14.8
All products	**2,235.5**	**1,563.1**	**1,827.1**	**2,057.5**	**1,849.8**	**1,634.5**

[a]Residue-related products include particleboard, chips, pulp and paper products, bioenergy products, decorative bark, and mill residues sold within and outside the state.

[b]Plywood and veneer sales included with lumber to prevent disclosure of firm level data.

through 2007 were approximately $1.83 billion in 2006 dollars. In 1978, sales totaled about $2.19 billion, followed by 1979 at almost $2.14 billion, and 1993 and 1994 at about $2.1 billion each (fig. 6). Total annual sales from Idaho's forest industry declined significantly, to around $1.5 billion, during 2008 and 2009 because of weak domestic housing and lumber markets and reduced consumption of other wood products during the recession (Brandt and others 2009,2010).

About 95 percent of primary wood products sales are concentrated in three sectors of the industry: sawmills, structural panels (i.e., plywood), and residue-related products. Residue-related products include particleboard, chips, pulp and paper products, bioenergy products, decorative bark, and mill residues. Sales values for residue-related products also include mill residue sold to users within Idaho as well as outside the state.

High sales values in the late 1970s were due in large part to strong lumber markets and high prices. Inflation-adjusted lumber sales from Idaho sawmills in the late 1970s exceeded $1 billion in 1977, and peaked in 1978 at nearly $1.5 billion. Sales values collapsed in the early 1980s with a severe recession, low production, and weak prices. Driven by 1982 lumber sales of just over $500 million, sales of all primary products that year totaled approximately $1.3 billion. In the last half of the 1980s, lumber sales moved back above $700 million and total sales was more than $1.6 billion.

Even though timber availability in Idaho limited production, 1993 and 1994 marked the first time since the late 1970s that total sales exceeded $2 billion and lumber sales exceeded $1 billion. As indicated earlier, 1993 and 1994 also had high wood product prices due to a strong U.S. economy and constrained timber availability on Federal lands throughout the Western United States. Sales value in the remainder of the 1990s fluctuated between $1.9 and $2.1 billion as lumber markets fluctuated. Consistently declining sales since 1999 have been due to lower per-unit prices as well as curtailments and closures. The lumber sales value of nearly $772 million in 2001 was the lowest since 1985 ($727 Million). To prevent disclosure of firm level information, sales data for lumber and other sawn products were combined with plywood and veneer sales totaling over $780 million dollars in 2006.

Total sales of all primary processors have been buoyed and stabilized to a degree by the expansion of the residue-utilizing sector. This sector has shown substantial increases in sales over the past 25 years and has become an increasingly important

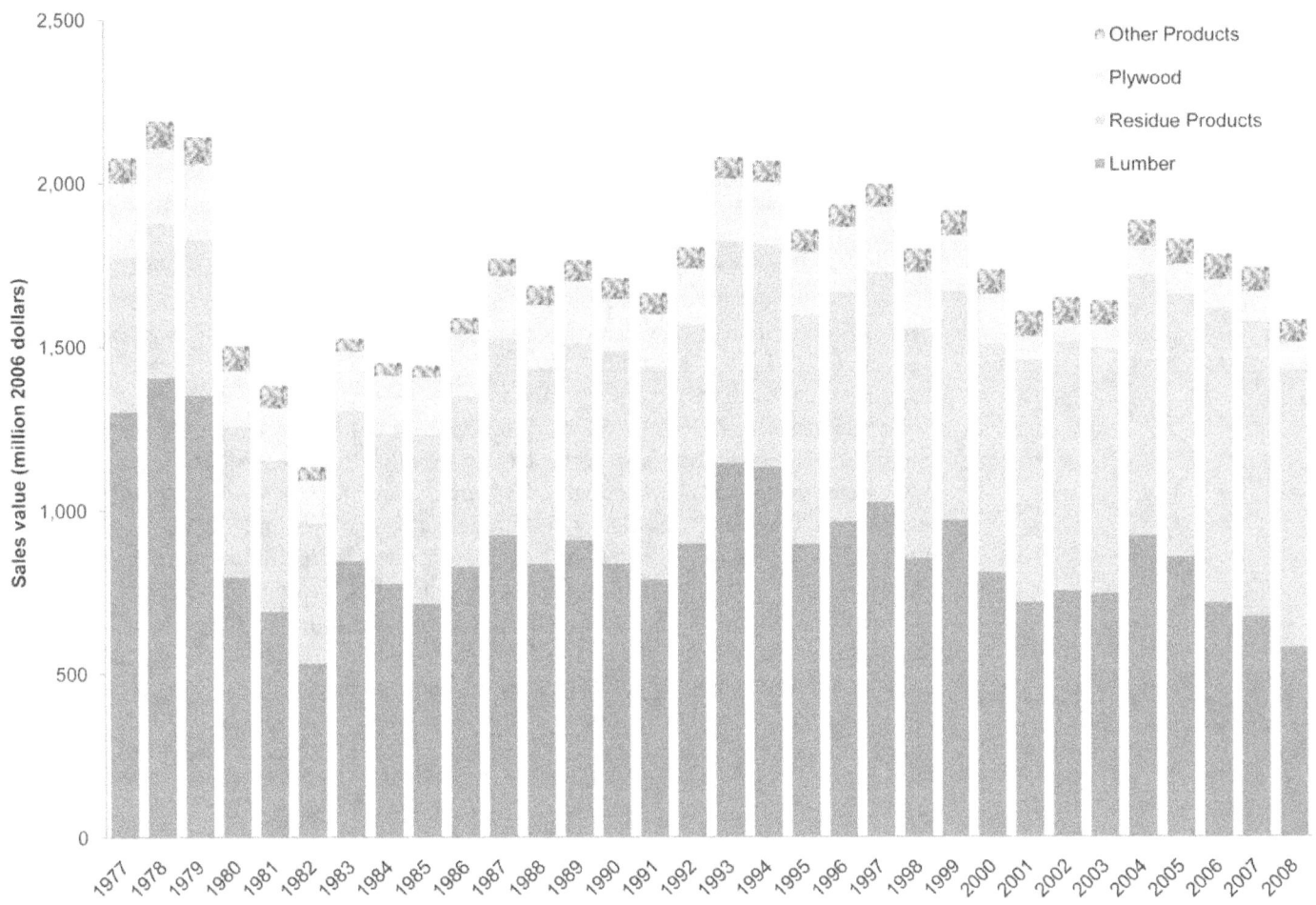

Figure 6—Sales value of Idaho's primary forest products, 1977 through 2007 (source: WWPA 1977-2007; Brandt and others 2009).

sector of Idaho's forest products industry. In order to avoid disclosure of firm-level data, published information was used to estimate a sales value for Idaho's residue-utilizing sector (DeKing 2004; Potlatch Corporation 2007; RISI 2007). Inflation-adjusted sales were about $625 million in 1979, versus $767 million in 2006. Sales by residue utilizing manufacturers currently account for about 47 percent of Idaho's forest industry sales, versus 28 percent in the late 1970s (fig. 6).

Structural panel sales, on the other hand, have contributed proportionately less to total sales than lumber. Structural panel sales peaked in 1978, with revenues of about $252 million. High prices brought sales to over $224 million in 1993 and 1994. Since 1997, weak plywood and veneer markets and a lack of available timber have led to plant closures. Only three plywood and veneer facilities remained in Idaho in 2006, the fewest since industry censuses began in 1979.

Sales by the remaining sectors of Idaho's primary wood products industry totaled over $86 million, the highest for any census year since the $96.5 million reported in 1979. While sales of cedar products and post and poles fell from 2001 to 2006, house log sales increased by nearly 8 percent.

USDA Forest Service Resour. Bull. RMRS-RB-12. 2012

19

Timber Received by Idaho Mills

Idaho mills received over 1,150 MMBF Scribner of timber for processing during 2006. Timber receipts refer to the volume of timber delivered to Idaho mills from in-state and out-of-state sources. Timber receipts for Idaho mills differ from the state's timber harvest because some timber harvested in Idaho was processed in other states, and some of the timber processed in Idaho was harvested outside the state.

Saw and veneer logs constituted the vast majority (91 percent) of Idaho's timber receipts, while logs used for other timber products— posts and poles, log furniture, pulpwood, and industrial fuelwood—accounted for 5 percent of receipts in 2006. The remaining 4 percent of timber receipts consisted of logs used in cedar products and house logs used by log home manufacturers.

Private lands supplied the majority of each timber product category, except house logs; National Forests were the leading supplier of timber to Idaho log home manufacturers (table 11). Industrial lands were the leading supplier of saw and veneer logs (480 MMBF) and also provided the majority of volume (32 MMBF) for other products in 2006. The majority, over 80 percent, of the timber received for other products was timber used in the manufacture of pulpwood and utility poles.

True firs were the leading species received by Idaho mills in 2006, accounting for 33 percent of receipts followed by Douglas-fir, which accounted for 30 percent of Idaho's timber receipts (table 12). True firs accounted for the largest proportion of sawlogs and veneer logs, as well as other products, while Spruce provided the largest proportion of house log receipts. Saw and veneer log receipts were the largest volume for each species.

Table 11—Idaho timber receipts by ownership class and product, 2006.

Ownership class	Saw and veneer logs[a]	House logs	Cedar products	Other products[b]	All products
	------------------- Thousand board feet, Scribner -----------------------				
Private	**797,044**	**1,526**	**13,909**	**39,002**	**851,481**
Industrial	480,373	285	8,789	31,922	521,369
Non-industrial private	313,391	1,241	5,120	6,160	325,912
Tribal	3,280	-	-	920	4,200
Public	**229,995**	**13,450**	**9,710**	**17,872**	**271,027**
Na ional Forest	52,610	12,526	500	3,924	69,560
Other public	177,385	924	9,210	13,948	201,467
Canadian and unspecified[c]	**23,918**	**2,024**	-	**1,701**	27,643
All owners	**1,050,957**	**17,000**	**23,619**	**58,575**	**1,150,151**

[a]Saw and veneer logs combined to prevent disclosure of firm level data.

[b]Other products include logs used for pulpwood, posts and poles, log furniture, and industrial fuelwood.

[c]Includes timber receipts from Canada and unspecified out-of-state sources.

Table 12—Idaho timber receipts by species and product, 2006.

Species	Saw and veneer logs[a]	House logs	Cedar products	Other products[b]	All products
	- Thousand board feet, Scribner -				
True firs	356,455	132	-	27,600	384,187
Douglas-fir	338,529	3,374	-	67	341,970
Cedar	97,398	306	23,619	23,733	145,056
Larch	66,338	125	-	-	66,463
Lodgepole pine	54,327	4,025	-	6,460	64,812
Ponderosa pine	49,077	2,758	-	683	52,518
Western hemlock	51,892	-	-	-	51,892
Spruce	19,905	6,198	-	19	26,122
Western white pine	16,163	30	-	-	16,193
Other species[c]	873	51	-	13	3,672
All species	**1,050,957**	**17,000**	**23,619**	**58,575**	**1,150,151**
	- Percentage of receipts -				
True firs	31.0	0.0	-	2.4	33.4
Douglas-fir	29.4	0.3	-	0.0	29.7
Cedar	8.5	0.0	2.1	2.1	12.6
Larch	5.8	0.0	-	-	5.8
Lodgepole pine	4.7	0.3	-	0.6	5.6
Ponderosa pine	4.3	0.2	-	0.1	4.6
Western hemlock	4.5	-	-	-	4.5
Spruce	1.7	0.5	-	0.0	2.3
Western white pine	1.4	0.0	-	-	1.4
Other species[c]	0.1	0.0	-	0.0	0.3
All species	**91.4**	**1.5**	**2.1**	**5.1**	**100.0**

[a]Saw and veneer logs combined to prevent disclosure of firm level data.

[b]Other products include logs used for pulpwood, posts and poles, log furniture, and industrial fuelwood.

[c]Other species include: redwood, red alder, quaking aspen, and other unknown species.

Sawmill Sector

Sawmills are the major component of Idaho's forest products industry in terms of sales output, plant numbers, and timber volume processed. In 2006, Idaho's 35 active sawmills continued to process the majority of the timber in the state and produced 1.8 billion board feet of lumber and other sawn products, representing 4.9 percent of the total U.S. production of softwood lumber (5.1 percent in 2001) and about 2.9 percent of the nation's softwood lumber consumption (3.4 percent in 2001).

The most common species used by Idaho's sawmill sector are Douglas-fir, true firs, western hemlock, western larch, western red-cedar, ponderosa pine, lodgepole pine, western white pine, and Engelmann spruce. High quality select and shop grades of lumber are produced, as are small volumes of structural timbers, but approximately 87 percent of production is dimension and stud lumber used for construction.

USDA Forest Service Resour. Bull. RMRS-RB-12. 2012

21

Changes in Lumber production

Driven by strong markets and increasing timber harvest, the period from 1947 to 1960 showed steady growth in lumber production. Harvest levels in Idaho prior to World War II on both public and private lands were relatively low in relation to timber inventories (Wilson and Spencer 1967). After World War II, public policy encouraged increased harvest on Federal lands to meet the strong national demand for building products, and improved markets also increased harvest on private lands (Flowers and others 1993). From 1947 to 1960, the volume of timber harvested from Idaho timberlands increased from under 1 billion board feet to nearly 1.5 billion, and virtually all of that timber was processed by sawmills (Setzer and Wilson 1970).

During the 1960s, lumber production showed little year-to-year variation, ranging from 1.6 to 1.7 billion board feet. Market conditions during that period were relatively stable with a strong U.S. economy and no recessions between 1960 and 1970. Lumber production remained stable despite the expansion of Idaho's plywood industry that used an increasing amount of timber that could have been processed into lumber. In less than 10 years, the plywood industry's timber use increased from less than 25 million board feet (MMBF) Scribner in 1960, to more than 250 MMBF in the last half of the 1960s. Lumber production was sustained during this period primarily by an increase in harvest levels. The total harvest in Idaho increased from 1.6 billion board feet at the beginning of the decade to over 1.8 billion board feet in the late 1960s.

Idaho's lumber production (fig. 7) clearly shows the influence of markets with a peak in the late 70's of nearly 2 billion board feet, followed by a sharp decline during the double dip recession of the early 1980s. However, Idaho lumber production was highest in 1989, at a time when markets were actually weaker than the in late 1970s. A 16 percent increase in lumber recovery per unit of log input between 1979 and 1990 was a major contributing factor to 1989's output of more than 2.1 billion board feet of lumber.

In the early 1990s, timber availability emerged as a major concern for the industry. Timber harvest fell nearly 15 percent by 1993 and lumber production was down nearly 10 percent from just over 2 billion board feet in 1990 despite very strong markets in 1993 and 1994. Prices in 1995 fell from the levels of the previous 2 years, and production fell to 1.67 billion board feet. In 1996, higher lumber prices increased production to 1.8 billion board feet. Prices continued to increase throughout the late 1990s, resulting in production of 1.86 billion board feet in 1999. Declining prices and further reductions in National Forest timber offerings led to decreased production in 2000 and 2001, with 2001 annual production totaling 1.8 billion board feet the lowest since 1996 (fig. 7).

Lumber production in 2006 was 1.85 billion board feet, 10 percent lower than production in 1990 (2.03 billion board feet) and 10 percent higher than in 1995 (1.66 billion board feet). Following 2006, Idaho's lumber production continued to decline and by 2008 had fallen 27 percent, producing just over 1.3 billion board feet. Idaho's estimated 2009 lumber production was 1.1 billion board feet. A number of factors impact lumber production from Idaho mills including:

- fluctuating housing and lumber markets
- timber availability
- increased recovery of lumber per board foot of log input

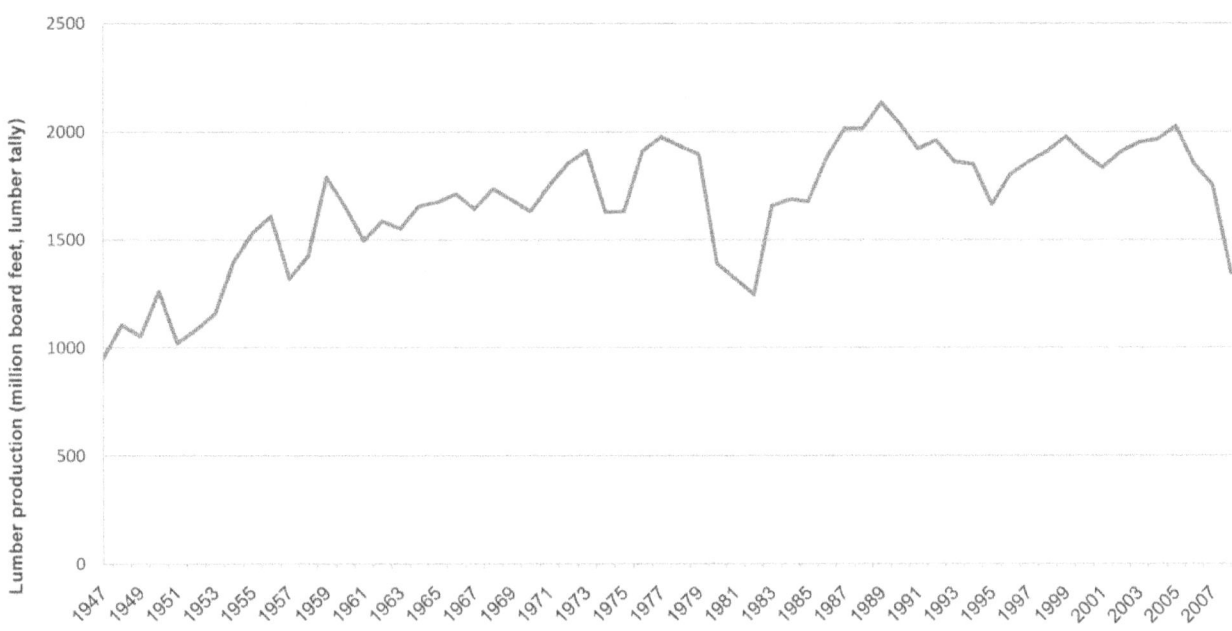

Figure 7—Idaho lumber production, 1947 through 2007 (source: WWPA 1964-2007).

- decisions by the industry to produce other products such as plywood instead of lumber, and
- log flows.

The combined harvest of saw and veneer logs in 2006 was 1,022 MMBF Scribner, 15 percent lower than in 1995 and 35 percent lower than in 1990. It is necessary to consider sawlogs and veneer logs when examining the impact of timber harvest on lumber production, because the plywood industry uses timber that also could be processed into lumber. Processing advancements between 1990 and 2006 allowed for increased lumber production per unit of log input thereby reducing the impact of declining harvest levels on lumber output. However, as total harvest has declined since 1990, the increased proportion of timber harvest utilized for lumber production has been the primary factor that has sustained lumber production in Idaho; this shift in timber allotted to lumber production is related to a commensurate reduction in timber available for plywood production.

Finally, demand for dimensional lumber weakened in 2006 following the recent housing boom that peaked in 2005 with new construction starts for single-family units (fig. 1). U.S. composite softwood lumber prices fell 16 percent from 2005 to an average annual price of 327 dollars per thousand feet of lumber tally in 2006, and continued to fall throughout 2007 and 2008 (Random Lengths 2009). Many Idaho sawmills have been negatively impacted by the falling lumber prices as a result of the downturn in housing. Stimson Lumber shut down its Atlas mill located in Coeur d'Alene in 2005 and later closed the DeArmond mill in 2008 citing poor market conditions related to the downturn in the housing market (Kramer 2005, 2008). North central Idaho also lost a sawmill in 2008 when Three Rivers Timber in Kamiah announced plans to shut down operations indefinitely due to low lumber prices and falling sales (Associated Press 2008).

Changes in lumber recovery—Between the 1979 and 1990 censuses, the volume of lumber recovered from 1 board foot Scribner of log volume increased from

Table 13—Idaho lumber recovery, selected years (sources: Keegan and others 1982,1988,1992,1997; Morgan and others 2004).

Year	Timber processed	Lumber produced	Recovery
	MBF[a] Scribner	MBF[a] Lumber tally	
1979	1,441,791	1,932,001	1.34
1985	1,224,540	1,665,375	1.36
1990	1,317,019	2,054,550	1.56
1995	1,074,090	1,643,359	1.53
2001	945,564	1,758,750	1.86
2006	953,432	1,805,113	1.89

[a]MBF = thousand board feet.

1.34 to 1.56 board feet lumber tally (table 13). Lumber recovery in Idaho has since increased to 1.89 board feet in 2006. Increases in recovery are due primarily to advances in technology and to decreased log diameter. The Scribner Decimal C log rule, which is used in Idaho, increasingly underestimates the amount of lumber that can be recovered as log diameter decreases, thus exaggerating lumber recovery per board foot of timber for smaller logs. Advances in production technology increase lumber recovery through computerized log scanning capabilities that identify optimum sawing patterns. Likewise, using thinner kerf saws and scanning equipment to edge and trim lumber have reduced the portion of the log that becomes sawdust.

Lumber production by geographic area—Information on lumber production at the sub-state level is currently available only through the ongoing censuses of Idaho's industry conducted by the BBER. Lumber output by county and region is discussed for census years, with an emphasis on recent changes, particularly since 1990. Idaho lumber production was 3 percent higher in 2006 than the previous census in 2001, 7 percent higher than 1995, and about 12 percent lower than in 1990 (table 14). The increased production since 1995 has been concentrated in the northern 10 counties while lumber production has continued to decline in the southern part of Idaho. The record high lumber production in northern Idaho is primarily due to increased recovery through technology upgrades at the mills and the decline of the plywood industry in northern Idaho. Since 1995, lumber production in Idaho's 10 northern counties has increased by 17 percent to 1.74 billion board

Table 14—Idaho lumber production by geographic area, census years 1979 through 2006 (sources: Keegan and others 1997, Morgan and others 2004).

County group	1979	1985	1990	1995	2001	2006
	-----------------MBF[a], lumber tally-------------------					
Bonner, Boundary	462,481	358,064	552,426	408,988	661,509	622,541
Benewah, Kootenai, Shoshone	467,965	490,866	629,129	613,014	563,482	591,446
Latah, Lewis, Nez Perce	360,847	198,633	262,148	213,610	274,990	290,619
Clearwater, Idaho	248,917	228,792	255,336	209,176	156,298	241,444
Northern Idaho	1,540,210	1,276,355	1,699,039	1,444,788	1,656,279	1,746,050
Southern Idaho	391,791	389,020	355,511	228,571	102,471	59,063
Idaho Total	1,932,001	1,665,375	2,054,550	1,673,359	1,758,750	1,805,113

[a]MBF = thousand board feet.

feet of lumber as production from mills in southern Idaho decreased by 74 percent to 59 million board feet.

County-level lumber production data are withheld to avoid disclosure of firm-level information. Bonner and Kootenai continued to be Idaho's top lumber producing counties in 2006, combining for over 809 MMBF of lumber production. Benewah, Nez Perce, and Idaho counties also accounted for a large portion of Idaho's lumber production, each producing over 180 MMBF, for a total of 591 MMBF in 2006.

Timber harvest on lands in northern Idaho increased by 8 percent since 2001, with a 14 percent increase in imports of saw and veneer logs from Canada and adjacent states. In addition, the decline of Idaho's plywood industry has increased the proportion of timber available to the sawmill sector.

The lumber industry in southern Idaho continued the downward trend that began in the late 1980s with a number of sawmill closures. Production in southern Idaho fell 42 percent from 2001 to 2006, 74 percent since 1995, and 83 percent since 1990. Mills in southern Idaho, which received more than 75 percent of their timber from National Forests in 1990 and over 60 percent in 1995 (Keegan and others 1992,1997), were more vulnerable to sharp declines in National Forest timber availability. Boise Cascade permanently closed its timber processing facilities during 2001, citing declines in Federal timber availability as the primary reason for the closures (Boise 2001).

Number and size of mills—The number of sawmills operating in Idaho has continued to decline over the last 50 years as production has become increasingly concentrated in a smaller number of large mills. The average output per mill continued to increase since the 2001 census and has increased nearly 10 fold since 1956, with the 2006 average annual output per mill at nearly 52 MMBF (table 15). The average annual output of Idaho mills nearly doubled between 1995 (27 MMBF) and 2001 (50 MMBF). Idaho timber processors with a capacity of over 50 MMBF accounted for over 94 percent of Idaho's timber processing capacity in 2006, compared to 61 percent in 2001, and just 39 percent in 1995. At the height of the post-World War II housing boom, there were more than 300, mostly small, sawmills in Idaho. Since then, the total number of mills had consistently declined until 2001. The 2006 census identified the same number of sawmills as 2001.

Although the total number of mills stayed the same in 2006, six fewer mills were identified in the 10 to 50 MMBF output size class and six additional mills were found to have produced less than 10 MMBF of lumber. The loss of several large

Table 15--Number of active Idaho sawmills by production size class and average annual lumber production, 2006.

Lumber production size class	Number of mills	Percentage of production	Lumber production	Average production per mill
			MBF[a]	MBF[a]
Over 100 MMBF	9	73.8	1,333,067	148,119
50 to 100 MMBF	5	20.3	367,218	73,444
10 to 50 MMBF	3	3.9	71,268	23,756
1 to 10 MMBF	9	1.8	31,675	3,519
Less than 1 MMBF	9	0.1	1,885	209
Total	35	100.0	1,805,113	51,575

[a]Production volume in thousand board feet (MBF) lumber tally.

processors was the result in-part of declining harvest on National Forest lands. Most of the small mills opened in southern Idaho since the 2001 census. These small mills represent less than 2 percent of the state's lumber production and are primarily supplied by timber from small scale forest management activities occurring locally on private lands. The 2006 census identified only 17 mills producing more than 10 MMBF annually—the fewest in the last 50 years (table 16).

As lumber production has become increasingly concentrated into larger facilities, ownership of the facilities has also consolidated as a result of several mergers of large forest products companies in Idaho. In 2001, the five largest forest products companies in Idaho produced 67 percent of the state's lumber production compared to 79 percent in 2006. Since 2006, these largest companies have further merged, and are currently controlled by just three entities.

Residue-Related Products Sector

In addition to products such as lumber and plywood, the processing of timber generates substantial volumes of wood fiber by-products. These by-products, referred to as mill residue, are the raw material source for the residue-related products sector. The 2006 census identified a total of 12 facilities in this sector, five fewer than in 2001. These included a pulp and paper mill and associated tissue plant, a particleboard plant, two wood fuel pellet producers, three facilities generating steam or electricity, and four facilities producing bark-related products such as decorative and landscape bark.

The total sales from the residue-related sector were $767 million in 2006, down nearly 16 percent from 2001 ($912 million), and down nearly 12 percent from1995 ($867 million). Although this sector has slightly declined since 2001, it remains a substantial part of Idaho's forest products industry, accounting for approximately 47 percent of Idaho's primary forest products sales in 2006, compared to just 28 percent in 1979. Increased sales in this sector are primarily from expansion of the pulp and paper component. There has also been growth in other residue using products in Idaho such as pelletized fuel, decorative bark, and residue used for generating steam or electricity.

Idaho has only one particleboard plant and one pulp and paper mill, which produces Kraft pulp, paperboard, and tissue. Published information was used to report production at these facilities. Particleboard production in 2006 was slightly higher than the previous census year at 68 million square feet (MMSF, ¾-inch basis) versus 67 MMSF in 2001, 68 MMSF in 1995, and 60 MMSF in 1990 (Keegan and others 1992; Potlatch 2007). Production of paperboard and tissue in Idaho was 542,000 tons compared to 533,000 tons in 2001, 424,000 tons in 1995, and 411,000 tons in 1990 (Keegan and others 1992; Morgan and others 2004).

Several Idaho firms operate plants producing electricity for sale through the burning of wood residue. These plants are associated with timber processing facilities and historically produced steam energy for in-house use. Many of these plants began to produce electricity for sale to outside markets in the early 1980s. There are other firms in Idaho that produce wood fuel pellets and bark products from the residues generated by timber processing facilities. Since 1988 the University of Idaho has been using sawmill residues to produce steam to heat the main campus in Moscow (Latah County), saving Idaho taxpayers upwards of $2 million per year, depending on the price of natural gas.

Plywood, Veneer, and OSB

In 2001, one of the four plywood/veneer plants operating in Idaho closed. To prevent disclosure of firm level information, production and sales information pertaining to the remaining three facilities operating in 2006 will not be reported. Production in 2001 was approximately 254 MMSF (3/8-inch basis) of plywood and veneer and had a total sales value of $69.9 million.

During the late 1950s and early 1960s, two plants producing plywood and veneer operated in Idaho with combined total production of less than 50 MMSF annually. The industry began to expand dramatically in the mid-1960s, with the construction of four new plants. Production reached 603 MMSF in 1967, which remained the highest level of production until the late 1980s. Slight expansion continued throughout the 1970s, and industry output remained between 500 and 600 MMSF annually. By 1979, eight plants producing structural panels or veneer were operating in Idaho. Production of structural panels decreased 200 MMSF during the recession years of the early 1980s and by 1985 two plywood plants and one plystran plant had closed. However, in 1984 an oriented strand board (OSB) plant was opened, raising the number of active plants in Idaho to six. The industry rebounded quickly from the recession and production increased to pre-recession levels by 1985, and peak production occurred in 1988 at 639 MMSF. The period from 1985 to 1995 was marked by stability in both the number of plants operating and production levels. All six plants operating in 1985 were still operating in 1995, and production remained stable at approximately 600 MMSF per year. In 1995, production approached the peak levels of 1988 at 637 MMSF.

In the late 1990s, the structural panel sector began a period of significant decline. The OSB plant closed in 1997, and a plywood plant closed in 2000, reducing the number of active structural panel plants operating in Idaho to four. Another plywood plant closed in 2001. The closures since 1995 were due to reduced timber availability, as well as increased competition from OSB producers elsewhere in North America and overseas.

Other Primary Manufacturers

The 2006 census identified 47 other active primary manufacturers processing timber into cedar products, log homes, utility poles, posts, and other small roundwood products such as corral poles, tree stakes, and roundwood log furniture. In 1995 and 2001, there were 79 and 53 facilities, respectively (table 9).

Posts, poles, and log furniture—In 2006, 16 plants in Idaho manufactured various types of roundwood products, such as utility poles, posts, corral poles, and log furniture. These plants had sales of $14.8 million from an output of nearly 1.5 million pieces, a decrease from 2001, when sales were $24.9 million from an output of approximately 2.3 million pieces and 22 facilities were operating (table 9 and 10). Sales of these products in 1995 were $32.9 million, and production was 3.7 million pieces with 32 plants operating.

Cedar products—Cedar product manufacturers processed nearly 24 MMBF Scribner of logs in 2006, down 26 percent from the 34 MMBF in 2001. Since 1979, the number of manufacturers for cedar products such as cedar shakes, shingles, split rail fencing, and fence lath in Idaho has steadily declined from 44 facilities to 26 in 1990, 10 in 2001, and 7 in 2006. Cedar product sales experienced a

USDA Forest Service Resour. Bull. RMRS-RB-12. 2012

27

decline from nearly $34 million in 1979 to under $14 million in 1985, $20.5, million in 1990, and $17.6 million in 1995. However, cedar product sales rebounded and reached their highest level ever at $34.1 million dollars in 2001 and declined slightly in 2006 to $33.5 million after adjusting for inflation. Most of this growth was in split cedar posts and rails and fence lathe as a result of higher prices and increased production of these products.

Log homes—The 2006 census identified 24 log home manufactures, an increase of three since 2001 and the only sector to see an increase in the number of facilities from 2001 to 2006. Idaho's log home sector recorded the highest level of sales on record with nearly $38 million dollars compared to the previous record of $28.6 million in 2001. While the log home industry still only accounts for just over 2 percent of Idaho's primary forest product industry sales, it has grown substantially since 1979. The 2006 census identified 24 log home manufacturers, producing over 3.2 million lineal feet of house logs. This compares to 1995 sales of $26.3 million and production of 3.7 million lineal feet. Sales and production in 1979 were $20.1 million and 4 million lineal feet, respectively. Sales increases from 1995 to 2006 were due to additional processing of house logs into complete building shells or homes, the use of higher value logs, and the design and production of higher value homes.

Plant Capacity

This section estimates the timber-processing capacity and the proportion of that capacity utilized by Idaho's primary forest products manufacturers in 2006. This analysis focuses on plants processing sawtimber: sawmills, plywood and veneer plants, house log plants, and utility pole plants. Capacity and utilization for the non-sawtimber processing manufacturers are discussed in less detail.

A Definition of Production Capacity

Mills were asked to specify production capacity—volume of finished product the facility is capable of producing both per eight-hour shift and annually given sufficient supplies of raw materials and firm market demand for products. Most of the larger mills estimated annual capacity based on two 8- or 10-hour shifts daily for a 220 to 260 operating days per year. A few facilities estimated annual capacity equivalent to operating 24 hours per day for 220 to 250 days per year. Smaller mills reported annual capacity at only one shift per day for not more than 250 operating days per year.

Capacity in Units of Raw Material for Sawtimber Processors

Sawtimber processors reported production capacity in a variety of units. Sawmills reported production capacity in thousand board feet lumber tally, while plywood capacity was reported in thousand square feet on a 3/8-inch basis. Utility pole production capacity was reported in numbers of pieces of a given size, and house log capacity in lineal feet. To combine the production capacity figures from different sectors and estimate the industry's total capacity to process sawtimber, production capacity was converted to units of timber input (MMBF Scribner) on a mill-by-mill basis, using each facility's product recovery factor. Sawmill capacity figures were adjusted to MMBF of timber by dividing production capacity in lumber tally by each mill's lumber recovery per board foot Scribner of timber processed. Plywood and veneer capacity figures were converted to MMBF Scribner by dividing production capacity in square feet by each mill's plywood recovery. Utility pole and house log capacities were adjusted to MMBF Scribner by multiplying capacity in the given finished product unit by an average Scribner board foot volume per piece or per lineal foot.

Industry's Capacity to Process Sawtimber, 1979 through 2006

Estimates of capacity to process sawtimber and the utilization of total capacity for 1979, 1985, 1990, 1995, 2001, and 2006 are based on complete censuses of Idaho's industry. For non-census years, mill capacities and utilization were estimated using information from industry directories, trade associations, and industry consultants (Ehinger 2009; Keegan and others 2006; Random Lengths 2001-2010; Spelter and others 2009; WWPA 1964-2010). Detailed capacity information is not available prior to the 1979 census. Idaho's sawtimber processing capacity has declined by 37 percent since 1979, with most of the decline occurring after 1990 (fig. 8). Between 1979 and 1990, capacity declined 14 percent and fell 27 percent to 1,294 MMBF by 2001. In 2003, several mill closures reduced capacity to less than 1,150 MMBF. Census data for 2006 indicates Idaho's sawtimber processing capacity to be approximately 1,300 MMBF. Capacity to process sawtimber in Idaho declined during 2007 and 2008, falling to approximately 1,100 MMBF, the lowest capacity in the past three decades.

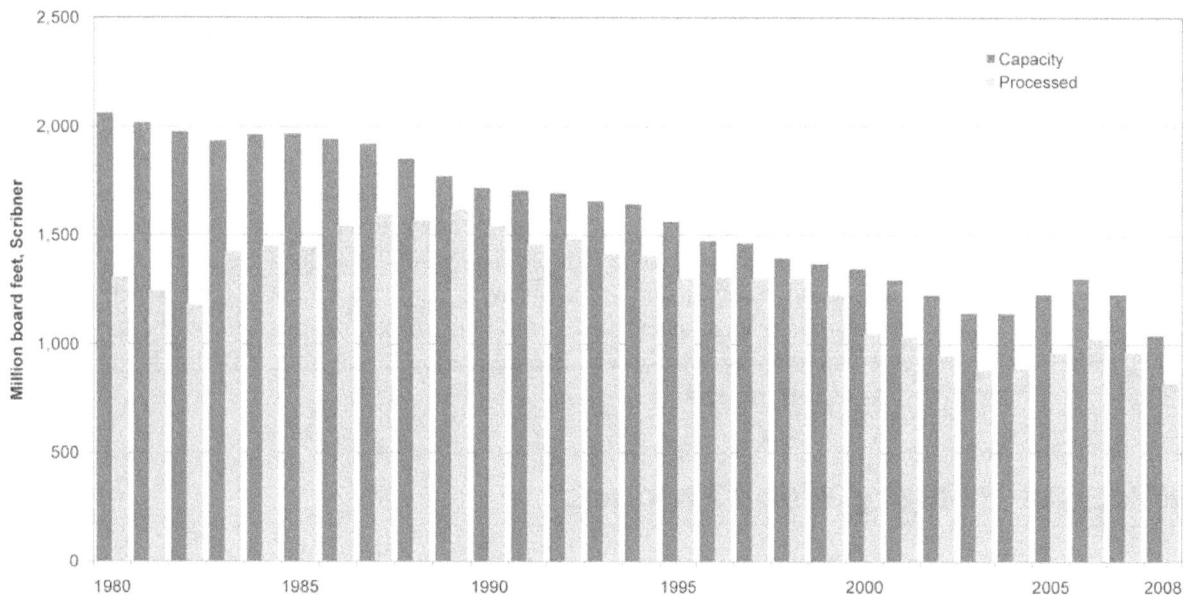

Figure 8—Idaho sawtimber processing capacity and sawtimber processed, 1979 through 2006 (source: Brandt and others 2009; Keegan and others 1997; Morgan and others 2004).

Sawtimber Capacity and Utilization by Sector

Although capacity to process sawtimber increased slightly from 2001 to 2006, utilization stayed about the same. Idaho mills processed 1,030 MMBF of saw timber, utilizing 79 percent of the state's capacity, the lowest level of utilization recorded since 1985 (table 17). Utilization peaked in 1990 at 90 percent before dropping to 83 percent in 1995 and 80 percent in 2001. During 2007 and 2008, utilization was approximately 79 percent and more mill closures are likely (Brandt and others 2009, 2010).

Idaho's overall capacity and utilization trend closely with the state's sawmill industry which accounted for 88 percent of sawtimber processing capacity in 2001 and a greater portion in 2006. The 2001 closing of an Idaho plywood plant required that estimates of plywood capacity and utilization be combined with sawmills to prevent disclosure of firm level information. The combined sawtimber capacity of sawmills and plywood and veneer plants in 2006 was 1,293 MMBF, slightly higher than the combined capacities in 2001 of 1,266 MMBF but 36 percent lower than in 1979. Utilization among these facilities in 2006 was about the same as in 2001 (about 80 percent) and in 1979 (81 percent). The increase in capacity in 2006 was the result of the addition of a northern Idaho sawmill. This was followed by the closing of two large sawmills in 2008, reducing the state's total capacity to less than 1,150 MMBF.

Idaho's plywood and veneer sector has experienced a significant decline since 1995. This sector's capacity fell from 202 MMBF in 1995 to 126 MMBF in 2001 as utilization dropped from 91 percent to just 57 percent. These estimates were the lowest on record and were indicative of a significant decline in Idaho's structural panel sector. The addition of an OSB plant and the closure of a plywood plant caused capacity to initially increase from 1979 to 1985, and then fall from 1985 to 1995. Since 1995, the structural panel sector has seen the closure of the OSB plant, and a plywood plant, reducing the sector's capacity by 76 MMBF. Capacity utilization for these facilities was 91 percent in 1995. Plywood and OSB plants tend to run at a higher rate of capacity utilization because they are more capital-intensive than the average sawmill, and their manufacturing processes are not easily shut down. A large part of the decline in capacity utilization in 2001 was due to one plant operating for less than half of the year and then closing permanently.

The annual timber processing capacity of Idaho's utility pole and house log sectors in 2006 was 11 MMBF, significantly lower than the 2001 census despite the increase in the number of house log plants. The decrease since 2001 was mainly due to the decline in the use of sawlogs to produce house logs, which can be made from logs of a lower quality. In 2006, 55 percent of sector capacity was utilized, which is somewhat lower than utilization levels from 2001 but higher than previous census years.

Markets for Primary Wood Products

This chapter examines the markets for Idaho's primary forest products industry and compares 2006 survey results with 1995 and 2001. Respondent mills summarized their 2006 shipments of finished wood products, providing information on volume, sales value, and geographic destination (fig. 9). Mills usually distributed their products through their own distribution channels or through independent

Figure 9—Shipment destinations for Idaho's primary wood products. Regions are Idaho (1), Far West (2), Rocky Mountain (3), North-Central (4), South (5), and Northeast (6).

wholesalers and selling agents. Because of subsequent wholesale and retail transactions, the geographic destination reported may not precisely reflect final delivery points of shipments. Market destination for the residue sector could not be released without revealing firm-level information.

Excluding mill residues and sales by the residue-utilizing sector, sales from Idaho's primary wood products industry totaled $867 million in 2006, down 8 percent from the 2001 sales total (table 18). Between 2001 and 2006, inflation adjusted sales decreased in every region except the Rocky Mountain States and North Central States.

Sales to purchasers in the Rocky Mountain States increased from $215 million in 2001 to $235 million in 2006, while export sales to North Central States increased from $185 million to $200 million for the same period. A comparison of sales values from 2006 to values from 2001 shows decreases in sales to all regions except for the Rocky Mountain and North Central, with substantial declines in Idaho (12 percent), Northeast States (39 percent), and the Far West (19 percent).

The major market areas for Idaho's primary wood products remain the Rocky Mountain and Far West States, as well as the North Central States. Nearly 85 percent of Idaho's 2006 primary wood product sales occurred in four market areas: Idaho, Far West, Rocky Mountain, and North Central (table 18). Sales to the Rocky Mountain States increased from 23 percent of total sales in 2001 to 27 percent in 2006 and from 20 percent to 23 percent in North Central States. Sales decreased from 24 percent to 21 percent in the Far West and from 10 percent to 7 percent in the Northeast.

Table 18—Destination and value of Idaho's 2006 primary wood products sales[a]. All values in 2006 dollars.(sources: Keegan and others 1982,1988,1992,1997; Morgan and others 2004).

Product	Idaho	Rocky Mountain	Far West	North-Central	Northeast	South	Other countries	Unknown	Total
				-------- Sales value in thousand 2006 dollars --------					
Lumber, timbers, other sawn products, plywood and veneer[b]	102,986	211,176	167,197	187,605	54,739	48,597	8,652	-	780,953
Posts, poles, and log furniture	3,626	1,077	7,488	947	7	7	1,612	-	14,764
House logs and log homes	9,619	17,577	3,948	4,654	1,225	397	444	-	37,864
Cedar products	1,868	4,952	3,279	6,865	1,532	14,970	39	-	33,505
2006 All products total	**118,099**	**234,782**	**181,912**	**200,071**	**57,503**	**63,971**	**10,747**	**-**	**867,086**
2001 Total	133,566	215,045	225,674	184,553	94,971	69,485	14,462	-	937,758
1995 Total	229,977	263,199	212,698	263,578	113,223	96,787	11,472	-	1,190,935
1990 Total	135,469	132,038	194,946	245,295	161,927	108,009	16,418	22,217	1,016,319
1985 Total	95,421	162,993	128,228	190,095	119,921	111,411	2,180	95,601	905,849
1979 Total	171,940	327,691	145,245	408,411	165,775	168,514	16,139	207,116	1,610,831
				-------- Percentage of total sales value by product --------					
Lumber, timbers, other sawn products, plywood and veneer[b]	13	27	21	24	7	6	1	-	100
Posts, poles, and log furniture	25	7	51	6	0	0	11	-	100
House logs and log homes	25	46	10	12	3	1	1	-	100
Cedar products	6	15	10	20	5	45	0	-	100
2006 All products total	**14**	**27**	**21**	**23**	**7**	**7**	**1**	**-**	**100**
2001 Total	14	23	24	20	10	7	2	0	100
1995 Total	19	22	18	22	10	8	1	0	100
1990 Total	13	13	19	24	16	11	2	2	100
1985 Total	11	18	14	21	13	12	0	11	100
1979 Total	11	20	9	25	10	10	1	13	100

[a] Does not include mill residue sales or sales by the residue-utilizing sector.

[b] Lumber, timbers, and other sawn products includes plywood and veneer sales value to prevent disclosure of firm level data.

Market Areas by Finished Product Type

Sales of Idaho's plywood, veneer, lumber, timbers, and other sawn products totaled just under $781 million in 2006; with sales to the Rocky Mountain States accounting for 40 percent of all sales—13 percent in Idaho and 27 percent to other Rocky Mountain States. Sales figures for these products were combined to prevent disclosure of firm level information. In 2001, these states accounted for 37 percent of sales for this product group. The Far West and North Central States accounted for 21 and 24 percent of 2006 sales, respectively. Sales to the Northeast decreased by 33 percent while sales to the South, and to other countries remained relatively stable since 2001.

The majority of Idaho's 2006 post, pole, and log furniture product sales were in Idaho and the Far West, accounting for 25 and 51 percent of post, poles, and log furniture sales, respectively. In 2001 sales to Idaho were slightly higher at 27 percent of sales while sales to the Far West States only accounted for 29 percent. Sales in other Rocky Mountain States remained stable, dropping from 8 percent in 2001 to 7 percent 2006.

Log home and house log manufacturers generated about $37.8 million in sales in 2006. Idaho and the other Rocky Mountain States, as well as the North Central States, were the major markets for these products, comprising 83 percent of total sales. Compared to 2001, sales increased in Idaho by 3 percent, by 4 percent in North Central States, and by 7 percent in other Rocky Mountain States. Sales decreased 12 percent in Far West States from 2001 to 2006. Sales of cedar products (including cedar shakes, shingles, and split rail fencing) generated about $33.5 million. The major markets for cedar products were the South and North Central States, with 45 percent of cedar sales going to the South and 20 percent to the North Central States. These two areas were also the major markets in 2001, accounting for 41 percent of cedar sales in the South and 22 percent of sales in the North Central States. Cedar exports, as well as sales to the Northeast States, have declined considerably since 1995, when those two market areas represented a combined 12 percent of total sales.

Mill Residue: Types, Quality, and Use

This chapter details the volumes and uses of mill residue generated by these plants. Wood fiber residue from primary wood products manufacturers (mill residue) is the major source of raw material for Idaho's pulp and paper and board industry, and an important source of fuel for all major sectors of the wood products industry. If not used, wood residue can create difficult and expensive disposal problems. Sawmills and plywood plants generate nearly 95 percent of the mill residue produced by Idaho's forest products industry.

Three general types of wood fiber residue are generated by Idaho's sawmills and plywood plants. *Coarse* or chippable residue consists of slabs, edgings, and trimmings from lumber manufacturing, log ends, pieces of veneer not suitable for manufacturing plywood, and plywood peeler cores not sawn into lumber. *Fine* residue consists of planer shavings and sawdust from sawmills and sander dust from plywood plants. And *bark* is the third general type of residue.

USDA Forest Service Resour. Bull. RMRS-RB-12. 2012

33

Table 19—Idaho sawmill residue factors, selected years (source: Keegan and others 1982,1988,1992,1997; Morgan and others 2004).

Type of residue	1979	1985	1990	1995	2001	2006
	- - - - - - - - - BDU per MBF lumber tally[a] - - - - - - - - - -					
Coarse	0.47	0.53	0.43	0.45	0.42	0.39
Sawdust	0.25	0.21	0.18	0.18	0.17	0.15
Planner shavings	0.22	0.20	0.15	0.15	0.13	0.09
Bark	0.30	0.19	0.18	0.18	0.20	0.20
Total	**1.24**	**1.13**	**0.94**	**0.96**	**0.92**	**0.82**

[a]Bone-dry unit (BDU = 2,400 lb of oven-dry wood) of residue generated for every 1,000 board feet of lumber manufactured.

Respondents to the 2006 census provided information on volume of residue generated, sales value, and uses. Residue volumes were reported in bone-dry units. A bone-dry unit equals 2,400 pounds of wood, oven-dry weight. In addition to residue quantity and disposition, statewide residue factors, which quantify the number of bone dry units of residue generated per MBF of lumber produced, were updated for Idaho sawmills based on the 2006 census (table 19).

Supply of Mill Residue

Idaho sawmills and plywood plants generated an estimated 1,519 thousand bone-dry units (MBDU) of manufacturing residue in 2006 (table 20), compared to 1,755 MBDU in 2001, and 1,822 MBDU in 1995 (table 21). The decrease in residue generated since 1990 has resulted from a combination of decreasing volumes of timber being processed and improving technology. With computer guided saws, thinner kerf saws, better planers, and better plywood lathes, technological improvements have led to lower residue factors through time (table 19).

The proportion of manufacturing residue that is utilized has increased dramatically since 1969, largely because of pulp and paper industry expansion and the opening of particleboard plants in the region, but also because of the increasing use of wood residue as a fuel to dry lumber and veneer and to generate electricity. In 1969, only 63 percent of mill residues in Idaho were used, increasing to 89 percent in 1979, 94 percent in 1985, 98 percent in 1990, 99 percent in 1995, and nearly 100 percent in 2001 and 2006 (table 21).

Table 20—Volume of wood residue generated by Idaho sawmills and plywood/veneer plants,2006.

Residue type	Wood residue			Percentage of type		Percentage of total
	Used	Unused	Total	Used	Unused	
	- - - - - - - - - Bone-dry units[a] - - - - - - - - - -			- - - - - - - - - Percent of total - - - - - - - - -		
Coarse	734,009	95	734,104	99.99	0.01	48
Fine[b]	427,927	36	427,963	99.99	0.01	28
Bark	356,789	214	357,003	99.94	0.06	24
Total	**1,518,725**	**345**	**1,519,070**	**99.98**	**0.02**	**100**

[a]Bone-dry unit (BDU = 2,400 b of oven-dry wood) of residue generated for every 1,000 board feet of lumber manufactured.

[b]Fine residue includes sawdust and planer shavings.

Table 21—Production and disposition of residues by sawmills and plywood/veneer plants, Idaho 2006 (sources: Keegan and others 1997; Morgan and others 2004).

Type of residue	Total utilized	Reconstituted products	Hogfuel	Other uses	Unused	Total
			- - - - - - - - - - - - - - *Thousand Bone Dry Units*[a] - - - - - - - - - - - - - -			
Coarse						
1979	987	957	10	20	21	1,008
1985	976	930	28	18	14	990
1990	1001	988	0	13	5	1,006
1995	885	872	3	10	1	886
2001[c]	806	773	30	3	3	810
2006	735	639	86	10	[b]	735
Sawdust						
1979	399	197	164	38	58	457
1985	308	176	115	17	22	330
1990	365	175	167	23	13	378
1995	306	158	133	15	4	310
2001	237	80	148	9	–	237
2006	266	224	40	2	[b]	266
Planer Shavings						
1979	340	215	112	13	20	360
1985	288	128	155	5	17	305
1990	310	221	88	1	9	319
1995	250	130	113	7	8	258
2001	307	193	113	1	[b]	307
2006	161	125	34	2	[b]	161
Bark						
1979	473	–	429	44	174	647
1985	282	–	263	19	73	355
1990	395	–	344	51	19	414
1995	358	–	343	15	10	368
2001	401	–	384	17	[b]	401
2006	357	–	333	24	[b]	357
Total						
1979	2,199	1,369	715	115	273	2,472
1985	1,854	1,234	561	59	126	1,980
1990	2,071	1,384	599	88	46	2,117
1995	1,799	1,160	592	47	23	1,822
2001[c]	1,751	1,046	675	30	3	1,755
2006	1,519	988	493	38	[b]	1,519

[a]Bone dry unit = 2,400 lb of ovendry wood.

[b]Less than one thousand bone dry units.

[c]Numbers do not sum to total due to rounding.

Coarse residue comprised the largest share of residues in 2006. Mills produced 734.1 MBDU, with nearly 100 percent (734.0 MBDU) utilized. Pulp and paper mills in Idaho and other states received 639 MBDU, with 95 MBDU going to other uses, primarily internal energy use. Less than 1 MBDU of coarse residue was unused in 2006 (table 21).

Of the 428 MBDU of fine residue used, over 80 percent (349 MBDU) went to pulp and paper mills or board plants for use as a raw material, 74 MBDU were consumed as fuel, and 5 MBDU went for other uses such as animal bedding, mulch, and raw material for other products. Table 21 further divides fine residues into planer shavings and sawdust. Planer shavings totaled 161 MBDU, while saw and sander dust totaled 266 MBDU.

Use of bark has increased dramatically since 1969 when only 39 percent was utilized; nearly 100 percent was utilized in 2006. Of the 357 MBDU produced in 2006, 333 MBDU were consumed as fuel (table 21), 2 MBDU were used for miscellaneous products including decorative bark, livestock bedding, and mulch; less than 1 MBDU was unused.

Residues from Other Manufacturers

The manufacture of utility poles, house logs, cedar products, posts, small poles, and roundwood furniture generates several types of residue, including bark, shavings and peelings, log ends, cull portions of logs, and slabs from log home manufacturers. In 2006, just over 14 MBDU of these residues were produced, and nearly 100 percent of this volume was used. Uses of these residues include livestock bedding, garden mulch, firewood, or other fuel.

The Forest Products Industry and the Idaho Economy

This section discusses employment and worker earnings trends in Idaho's primary and secondary forest products industry as well as the industry's place in the economy of Idaho and northern Idaho. This analysis focuses on 2006 and 2007 (the most recent years for which comprehensive state and county economic data are available) and previous years. However, a dramatic downward shift in wood and paper markets occurred in 2006 with further steep declines and very poor markets in 2007 to 2009. The collapse of the U.S. housing industry and related global financial crisis in 2008 had a substantial negative impact on Idaho's forest products industry. For this reason, statewide employment and labor income estimates are provided at the state level for 2008 and 2009.

The primary forest products industry includes: logging; processing logs into lumber and other wood products; processing wood residues into outputs such as paper or electricity; and private-sector timber management services. The secondary industry, as defined in this report, includes the further processing of the outputs from the primary industry manufacturers either from Idaho or elsewhere. Portions of the secondary industry, such as truss and cut-stock manufacturers are directly linked and highly integrated with Idaho's primary industry. Other components such as mobile home manufacturers have limited links to and dependence on Idaho's primary industry.

Data from several sources were used to identify employment and labor income for Idaho's primary and secondary forest products industry, including the U.S.

Department of Commerce, Regional Economic Information System (REIS) (U.S. Department of Commerce 2009), along with wage and salary data from the U.S. Department of Labor, Bureau of Labor Statistics (U.S. Department of Labor 2009), the U.S. Census Bureau's County Business Patterns (U.S. Census Bureau 2009a), Idaho Department of Labor and information from the periodic censuses of the industry done by the Bureau of Business and Economic Research as part of the FIDACS system (Keegan and others 1982,1988,1992,1997; Morgan and others 2004).

Most of the primary and secondary industry is reported in four North American Industrial Classification (NAICS) sectors, as defined by the U.S. Office of Management and Budget (OMB 1998):

113	forestry and logging;
1153	support activities for forestry;
321	wood products manufacturing; and
322	paper manufacturing.

These classifications were used to estimate total employment and workers' earnings (labor income) in Idaho's forest products industry. This grouping of industry categories provides a conservative measure of the forest products or wood and paper products industry. However, a number of activities are not included in these classifications, including the hauling of logs by independent truckers; hauling of finished products by truck, rail or barge; and forest management activities by government employees. Additionally, a portion of the secondary industry—the manufacturing of wood furniture—is found in NAICS 337.

Based on these classifications, approximately 15,400 workers, earning over $750 million (in 2006 dollars), were employed in the forest products industry in Idaho in 2006. The primary sectors accounted for approximately 9,400 workers, while the secondary sectors employed the remaining 6,000.

Trends in Forest Products Employment and Labor Income

This section focuses on trends in Idaho forest industry employment since 1990; a discussion of longer term trends is in Morgan and others (2004). Note that the U.S. Department of Commerce used a different system prior to 2001 —the Standard Industrial Classification (SIC) system—to report economic statistics such as employment by industry (OMB 1987). SIC categories differ somewhat from the current NAICS categories, and employment and labor income prior to 2001 are not exactly comparable to post 2001.

The U.S. Department of Commerce developed a time series beginning in 1990 that translates the SIC data to NAICS classifications and this data series is used in this trend analysis. The reader should be aware that the trend in the 1990s under the modified NAICS data differs somewhat from the trend observed under the SIC system and reported in Morgan, and others (2004). The authors think that the combined NAICS and SIC data set does accurately reflect general changes in employment and labor income from the 1990s to the present and is used as the basis for this discussion of trends in employment and labor income. The years 1990 and 2006 offer fairly consistent points of comparison around which to frame a discussion of the forest products industry's impact on the Idaho economy and trends in employment and labor income. Both were years of modest but deteriorating demand for wood and paper products. Both years were followed by official recessions with the 1991 recession being relatively mild and short lived and followed by very strong market years through much of the 1990s, especially 1993 and 1994. The recession which began in 2007 and continued into 2009 has been the most severe and long lasting of the post-WW II recessions.

Employment—The wood and paper products industry is a substantial and relatively high paying industry in Idaho. Even with the severe economic conditions of the last several years Idaho's industry directly employed nearly 11,000 workers in 2009. The operations of the industry and spending and re-spending by its workers support an equal number of workers in other sectors of Idaho's economy (Cook and O'Laughlin 2006). In addition to generating considerable employment in other sectors, wood and paper workers earned an average of $49,000 in labor income for 2009; this is substantially more than the state average of $38,100 per worker.

Between 1990 and 2007, the number of workers in Idaho's wood and paper products industry declined by approximately 3,400 workers, from 18,440 in 1990 to 15,050 workers in 2007 (fig. 10). With the collapse of the U.S. housing industry and the related 2008 global financial crisis, employment in Idaho's wood and paper products industry dropped to an estimated 12,600 in 2008 and approximately 11,000 in 2009.

Idaho's primary and secondary industries had substantially different trends in employment. Primary employment dropped from 15,122 in 1990 to 9,300 in 2005 and 2006 and then to 8,100 in 2008. The major factors leading to the long term decline in primary industry employment was the nearly 35 percent reduction in timber harvest between 1990 and 2006 driven by an 80 percent decline in the Federal timber sale program in Idaho. The collapse of the U.S housing market impacted Idaho's primary industry beginning in 2006 and was the primary factor leading to the further fall off in employment in 2007 and 2008.

Both the primary and secondary industry benefited when generally strong economic performance globally, nationally, regionally, and in Idaho yielded strong demand for wood products through much of the 1990s and in 2004 and 2005. However, the secondary industry did not suffer from the sharply constricted raw material supply that plagued the primary industry. Most of the secondary industries use wood products manufactured by Idaho's or the region's primary industry as their input, but it only consumes a fraction of what the regional primary industry produces. Additionally, the secondary industry can more easily acquire raw materials from elsewhere. It is, therefore, not as susceptible to local declining timber availability as is the primary industry.

Overall wood and paper products employment actually increased from 1990 to 1999 from 18,442 to 19,314. The overall increase in the 1990s came about because secondary wood and paper employment increased by nearly 70 percent from 3,300 to 5,600 workers. At the same time, declines in the primary segments in the 1990s were proportionately less than the reduction in timber harvest with a 23 percent drop in timber harvest involving only a 10 percent decline in primary employment (15,100 to 13,700 in 1999). The increased labor intensity in the primary industry was due to a mix of factors including a number of very strong market years, which allowed expanded use of lower quality timber and increased utilization of processed logs.

The increase in employment per unit volume of timber harvested in Idaho's primary industry that occurred in the 1990s did not continue into the 2000s and primary employment dropped by one-third between 2000 and the high market year of 2005, while harvest volumes in Idaho declined by 6 percent over that period. Much weaker markets led to further declines in employment in 2006 to 2008, with

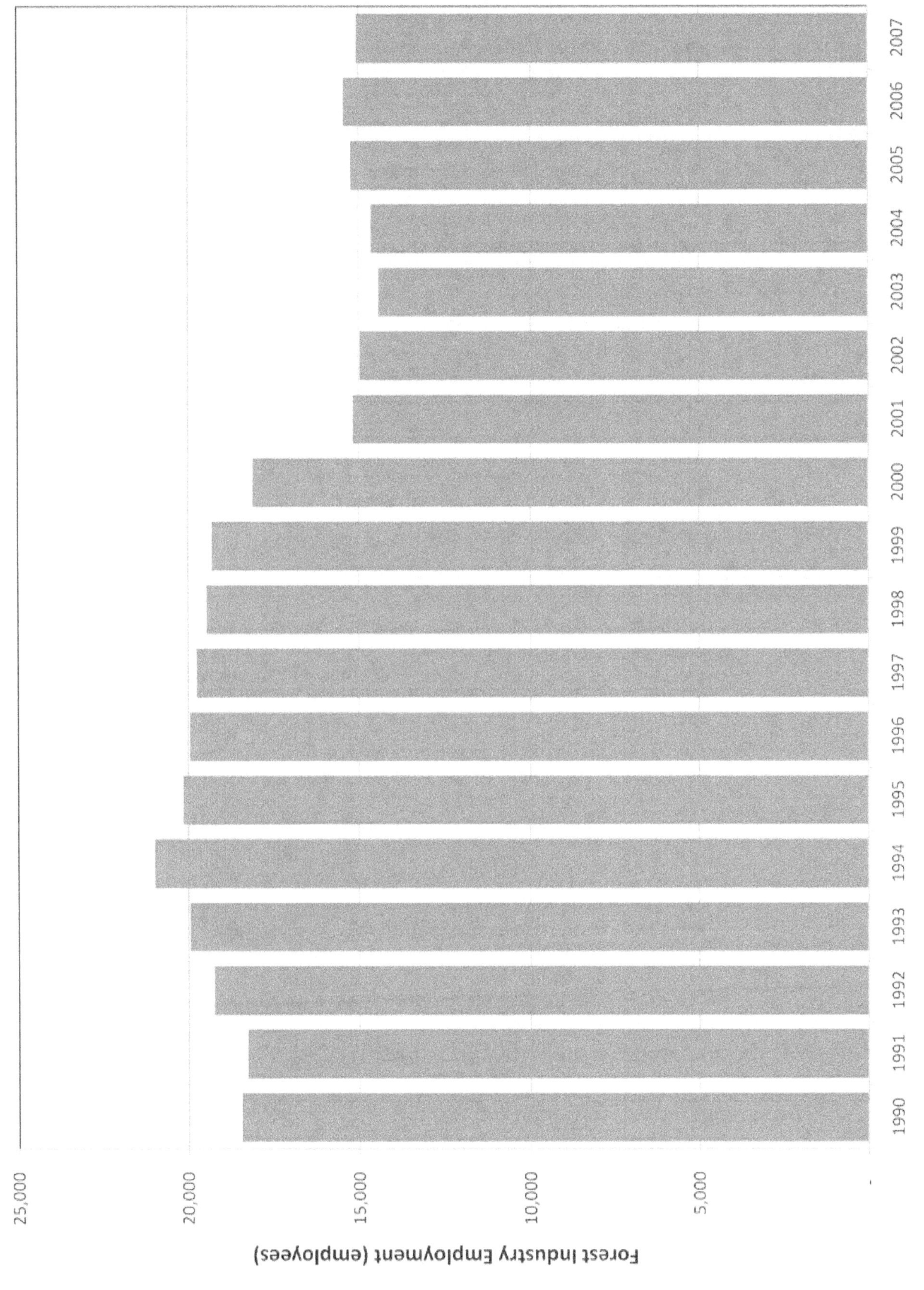

Figure 10—Idaho forest industry employment, 1990 through 2007 (source: U.S. Department of Commerce 2009).

USDA Forest Service Resour. Bull. RMRS-RB-12. 2012

39

primary employment falling to under 9,000 in 2008. The secondary industry continued to increase employment after 2000 to approximately 6,000 workers in 2006 and 2007. With much poorer economic conditions in 2008, secondary employment declined to an estimated 5,400 workers.

Labor Income—Labor income, or workers earnings, is the compensation that is financial compensation for work effort; including labor earnings, employer-provided benefits, taxes paid to the government on behalf of employees, and the portion of entrepreneurial income that is a return to labor. In this analysis labor income is used as a measure of the economic output of the state and counties or county groups within Idaho. Gross county product data are not readily available for Idaho, and labor income provides a consistent measure of economic activity at both the state and sub-state level. Labor income by industry group is available for each county and has proved to be a reasonable proxy for gross state and county product (Polzin 1990,2006; Polzin and others 1988). Because of the construction of the data sources it is not possible to distinguish between labor income earned by workers in the primary and secondary industry and, therefore, the discussion will deal with the entire wood and paper products industry. Similar to employment, labor income increased in the 1990s from $823 million to $1.0 billion in 1999 and with the accelerated loss of primary forest industry workers, labor income declined steadily from 2000 through 2008 dropping to $793 million in 2007 and approximately $700 million in 2008 (fig. 11).

The Forest Products Industry and Idaho's Economic Base

The structure of the Idaho and northern Idaho economies are reported in the context of an economic base approach. The economic base of a region consists of industries whose economic activity is dependent on factors external to the state or local economy. These "basic" industries are important to an economy because they have the potential to inject new funds by way of payrolls, taxes, and purchases of local goods and services. Changes in these industries have a strong influence on trends in the overall economy because they also stimulate changes in the derivative or non-basic sectors (Polzin 1990, 2006; Polzin and others 1988).The derivative sectors are composed of firms that depend largely on local business conditions, that is, they sell their products to local households, businesses, and individuals. Almost all local services (like drycleaners, grocery stores, and restaurants) are identified as non-basic because they depend almost entirely on local factors. Basic industries tend to be more insulated from local economic fluctuations since their products or services are generally sold in outside markets or they are otherwise dependent on outside funds.

By necessity, this analysis of the economic base is done on an industry basis; a more detailed analysis would require firm-level data to make reasonable geographic allocations of sales to identify basic components of the derivative industries. Available data do not allow for a perfect delineation of basic and derivative sectors, and in some cases this leads to an understatement of the economic base. For example, construction is not included as a basic industry at the state level. Much of construction is a derivative activity as illustrated by home building by Idaho residents. Portions of construction, such as federal highway funding, second home construction by non-residents, and plant construction or expansion by basic industries would be basic construction activities. There are also basic components of the service sectors, such as retail trade, finance, insurance, and real estate (F.I.R.E.) selling goods, services and real property to buyers outside of Idaho.

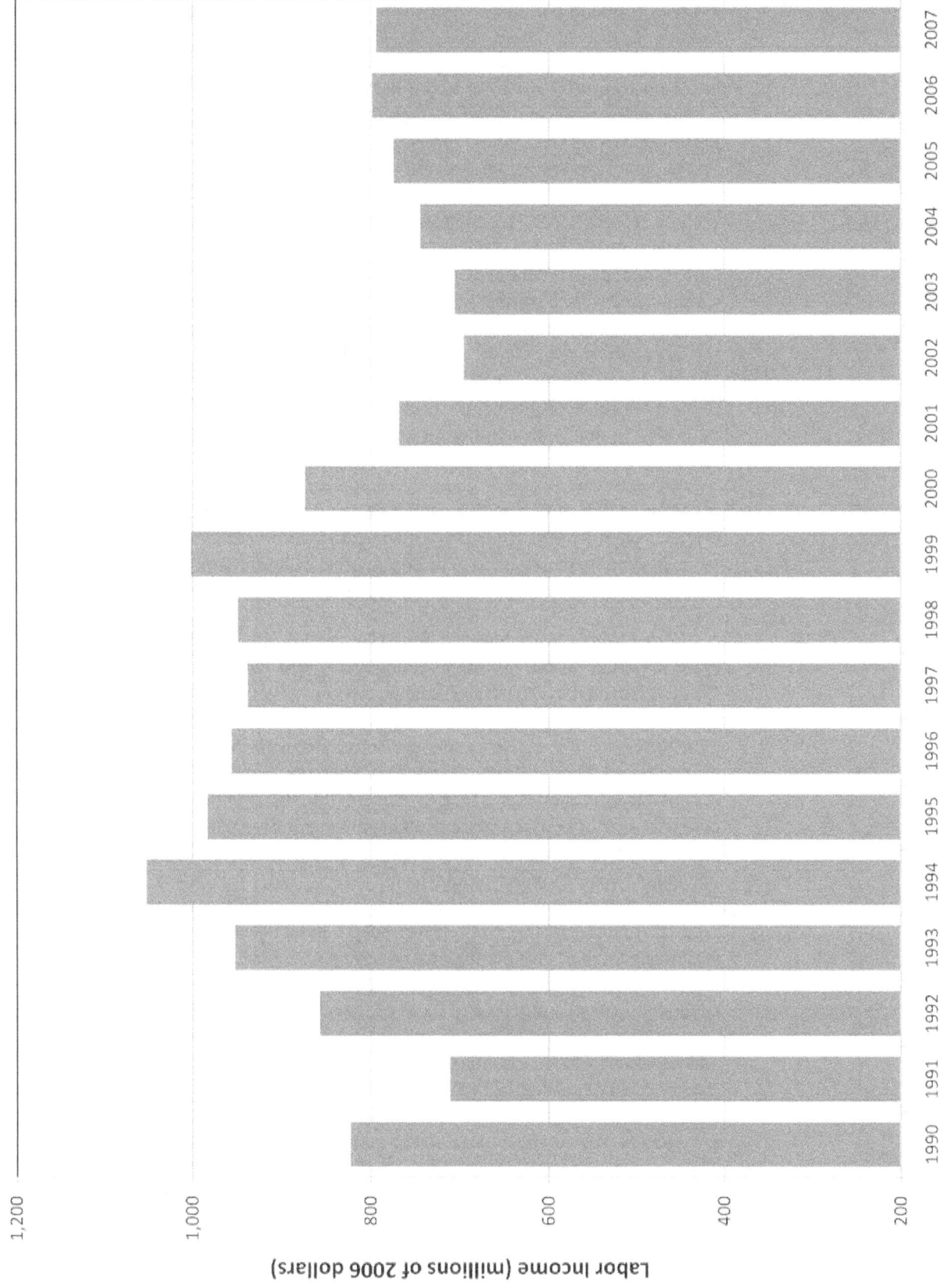

Figure 11—Idaho's forest industry adjusted labor income, 1990 through 2007 (source: U.S. Department of Commerce 2009).

USDA Forest Service Resour. Bull. RMRS-RB-12. 2012

41

The need to identify basic industries at a fairly broad scale can also result in some derivative activities being classified as basic, for example, products manufactured in Idaho that are sold at the retail level to Idaho residents. On balance, the directions of the basic industries identified in this report have been a major determinant of the direction of Idaho's and northern Idaho's economy over the past several decades (Polzin 1990, 2006; Polzin and others 1988).

The major basic industries in Idaho are agriculture, manufacturing (which is presented as food and kindred products), wood and paper products (much of which is also manufacturing), and all other manufacturing, nonresident travel, mining and transportation, and the Federal government. In 2007 over 70 percent of Idaho's economic base was natural resource related industries (agriculture, wood and paper products, non-resident travel, food processing) and/or manufacturing, both of which are components of the forest products industry (U.S. Department of Commerce 2009). Manufacturing, other than wood and paper products, and food processing, accounts for about 32 percent of Idaho's basic labor income, agriculture accounts for 18 percent, wood and paper products, food processing, and nonresident travel account for 8 percent each. The Federal government (civilian and military) is about 18 percent of earnings in basic industries with mining and transportation combined accounting for about 11 percent. The contribution of the wood and paper products industry to Idaho's economic base has declined proportionately over the last two decades from about 13 percent in 1990 to 8 percent in 2007. The proportionate decline has come about due to the modest drop in wood and paper products labor income from 1990 of about $35 million 2006 dollars, coupled with labor income increases of $1.9 billion in other manufacturing and a $600 million labor income increase in Federal government.

Northern Idaho's Economic Base—The forest products industry is substantially more important in the ten Idaho counties north of the Salmon River (Benewah, Bonner, Boundary, Clearwater, Idaho, Kootenai, Latah, Lewis, Nez Perce, and Shoshone counties) than in the state as a whole. Measured by labor income, less than 20 percent of the state's economic activity is in northern Idaho, however, $420 million out of $743 million in forest industry labor income (57 percent) is in these northern Idaho counties. Further, 87 percent of Idaho's timber harvest is from these counties, and virtually all of the wood and paper industry in northern Idaho is part of the primary forest products industry and directly engaged in harvesting, managing and processing timber products.

In addition to the state-level basic industries of agriculture, non-wood and paper products manufacturing, the forest products industry, nonresident travel, mining and transportation, and the Federal government, net retirement income and earnings of commuters living in northern Idaho but working elsewhere contribute measurably to the economic base in these ten counties. Despite declines in the last two decades, the forest products industry remains a major economic force in the region and remains the largest component of northern Idaho's economic base with labor income of $420 million in 2006 accounting for just over 23 percent of total worker earnings in basic industries (U.S. Department of Commerce 2009). In 1990 the forest products industry accounted for 39 percent of labor income in basic industries. The reduced share of northern Idaho's economic base is attributable to a decrease in the forest products industry labor income of about $93 million (constant 2006 dollars) and substantial increases in other manufacturing, net retirement income, and earnings of commuters, particularly those in the Kootenai County area working in eastern Washington.

Other manufacturing increased from $109 million in 1990 to $267 million in 2006 and northern Idaho residents working outside the area generated an inflow of $252 million in labor income in 2006, up from $57 million in 1990. Retirement payments represented a net inflow of over $213 million in 2006, or 12 percent of the economic base, up from $45 million in 1990 and 3.5 percent of the economic base.

References

Associated Press. 2008. Idaho saw mill to close as lumber demand shrinks. KTVB News. Nov. 7, 2008. Available online at www.ktvb.com/news/business/stories/ktvbn-nov0708-kamiah_mill_closes.18cbada0a.html. Last accessed Dec. 2, 2008.

Boise. 2001. Plywood, lumber operations in Idaho to close. Available online at www.prnewswire.com/cgi-bin/stories.pl?ACCT=105&STORY=/www/story/02-13-2001/0001426962. Last accessed Dec. 5, 2008.

Brandt, J.P.; Morgan, T.A.; Keegan, C.E., III; Wagner, F.G.; Shook, S.R. 2008. Idaho's forest products industry: Current conditions and forecast 2008. University of Idaho. Station Bulletin 89. 4 p.

Brandt, J.P.; Morgan, T.A.; Keegan, C.E., III; Wagner, F.G.; Shook, S.R. 2009. Idaho's forest products industry: Current conditions and forecast 2009. University of Idaho. Station Bulletin 92. 4 p.

Brandt, J.P.; Morgan, T.A.; Keegan, C.E., III; Wagner, F.G.; Shook, S.R. 2010. Idaho's forest products industry: Current conditions and forecast 2010. University of Idaho. Station Bulletin 96. 4 p.

Cook, P.S.; O'Laughlin, J. 2006. Idaho's forest products business sector: Contributions, challenges, and opportunities. University of Idaho, College of Natural Resources, Policy Analysis Group. Report No. 26, 48 p.

DeKing, Noel, ed. 2004. Pulp and paper global fact and price book 2003-2004: Incorporating the Pulp & Paper North American Factbook and the PPI International Fact & Price Book. San Francisco, CA: Paperloop, Inc. 311 p.

Ehinger, P.F. 2009. Personal communication. Consulting Forester, Paul F. Ehinger & Associates, 2300 Oakmont Way, #212, Eugene, OR 97401.

Fins, L.; Byler, J.; Ferguson, D.; Harvey, A.; Mahalovich, M.; McDonald, G.; Miller, D.; Schwandt J.; Zack, A. 2001. Return of the giants: Restoring white pine ecosystems by breeding and aggressive planting of blister rust-resistant white pines. Station Bull. 72. Moscow, ID: University of Idaho, College of Natural Resources. 20 p.

Flowers, P.J.; Conner, R.C.; Jackson, D.H.; Keegan, C.E., III; Long, B.; Schuster, E.G.; Wood, W.L. 1993. An assessment of Montana's timber situation. Misc. Pub. 53. Missoula, MT: The University of Montana, School of Forestry, Montana Forest and Conservation Experiment Station. 49 p.

Godfrey, E.B.; Schuster, E.G.; Bell, E.F. 1980. Idaho's forest products industry, 1973. Gen. Tech. Rep. INT-80. Ogden, UT: U.S. Department of Agriculture, Forest Service, Intermountain Forest and Range Experiment Station. 42 p.

Haminishi, C.M.; Wagner, F.G.; O'Laughlin, J.; Gorman, T.M. 1995. Idaho timber harvest projections by ownership to 2000: An issue-based survey of resource managers. Western Journal of Applied Forestry. 10(3):109-113.

Keegan, C.E., III; Jackson, T.P.; Johnson, M.C. 1982. Idaho's forest products industry: A descriptive analysis 1979. Missoula, MT: The University of Montana, Bureau of Business and Economic Research. 98 p.

Keegan, C.E., III; Martin, K.J.; Johnson, M.C.; Van Hooser, D.D. 1988. Idaho's forest products industry: A descriptive analysis 1985. Missoula, MT: The University of Montana, Bureau of Business and Economic Research. 90 p.

Keegan, C.E., III; Morgan, T.M.; Gebert, K.M.; Brandt, J.P.; Blatner, K.A.; Spoelma, T.P. 2006. Timber-processing capacity and capabilities in the Western United States. Journal of Forestry. 104(5):262-268.

Keegan, C.E., III; Wichman, D.P.; Van Hooser, D.D.; Gorman, T.M.; McClintick, M.W.; Polzin, P.E. 1992. Idaho's forest products industry: a descriptive analysis 1990. Missoula, MT: The University of Montana, Bureau of Business and Economic Research. 51 p.

Keegan, C.E., III; Wichman, D.P.; Van Hooser, D.D.; Gorman, T.M.; Wagner, F.G.; Polzin, P.E.; Hearst, A.L. 1997. Idaho's forest products industry: A descriptive analysis 1979-1996. Missoula, MT: The University of Montana, Bureau of Business and Economic Research. 68 p.

Kramer, B. 2005. Atlas Mill in Coeur d'Alene to close. Spokesman Review. Oct. 14, 2005. Available online at www.spokesmanreview.com/breaking/story.asp?ID=5146. Last accessed Dec. 3, 2008.

Kramer, B. 2008. Sawmill's final notes resonate. Spokesman Review. May 9, 2008. Available online at www.spokesmanreview.com/local/story.asp?ID=243982&page=all. Last Accessed Dec. 3, 2008.

Morgan, T.A.; Keegan, C.E., III; Hayes, S.W.; Sorenson, C.B.; Shook, S.R.; Wagner, F.G.; O'Laughlin, J. 2011. Idaho's forest products industry current conditions and 2011 forecast. Station Bulletin 97. Moscow, ID: Idaho Forest Wildlife and Range Experiment Station. 4 p.

Morgan, T.A.; Keegan, C.E., III; Spoelma, T.P.; Dillon, T.; DeBlander. 2004. Idaho's forest products industry: A descriptive analysis. Resour. Bull. RMRS-RB-4. Fort Collins, CO: U.S. Department of Agriculture, Forest Service, Rocky Mountain Research Station. 31 p.

Office of Management and Budget [OMB]. 1987. Standard industrial classification manual. Springfield, VA: Executive Office of the President. 705 p.

Office of Management and Budget [OMB]. 1998. North American industrial classification system. Lanham, MD: Executive Office of the President. 1247 p.

Polzin, P.E. 1990. The verification process and regional science. The Annals of Regional Science. 24:61-67.

Polzin, P.E. 2006. Strong economic growth continues in Montana. Montana Business Quarterly., 44(1): 8-20.

Polzin, P.E.; Connaughton, K.; Schallau, C.H.; Sylvester, J.T. 1988. Forecasting accuracy and structural stability of the economic base model. The Review of Regional Studies. 18:23-36.

Potlatch Corporation. 2007. 2006 Annual report. Available online at www.media.corporate-ir.net/media_files/irol/10/100877/AR06.pdf. Last Accessed Nov. 19, 2008.

Random Lengths. 1976-2009. Random Lengths yearbook: Forest product market prices and statistics. Eugene, OR: Random Lengths Publications, Inc.

Random Lengths. 2001-2010. Big book: The buyers and sellers directory of the forest products industry. Eugene, OR: Random Lengths Publications, Inc.

Random Lengths. 2008. U.S.-Canada trade dispute timeline 1982 to present. Eugene, OR: Random Lengths Publications, Inc.

Resource Information Systems Inc. [RISI]. 2007. Lockwood-Post directory of pulp & paper mills 2007. Boston, MA: Resource Information Systems, Inc. 541 p.

Setzer, T.S.; Wilson, A.K. 1970. Timber products in the Rocky Mountain States, 1966. Resour. Bull. INT-9. Ogden, UT: U.S. Department of Agriculture, Forest Service, Intermountain Forest and Range Experiment Station. 89 p.

Spelter, H.; Mckeever, T.; Toth, D. 2009. Profile 2009: Softwood sawmills in the United States and Canada. Res. Pap. FPL-RP-659. Madison, WI: U.S. Department of Agriculture, Forest Service, Forest Products Laboratory. 73 p.

U.S. Census Bureau. 2008. Manufacturing, mining, and construction statistics. Quarterly starts and completions by purpose and design. Available at www.census.gov/const/ www/quarterly_starts_completions.pdf. Last accessed April 2010.

U.S. Census Bureau. 2009a. County business patterns. Available online at http://www.census.gov/econ/cbp/index html. Last accessed April 2010.

U.S. Census Bureau. 2009b. New residential construction (building permits, housing starts, housing completions). Available at http://www.census.gov/const/www/ newresconstindex html. Last accessed April 2010.

U.S. Department of Commerce, Bureau of Economic Analysis. 2009. Regional accounts data. Available online: www.bea.gov/bea /regional/spi. Last accessed April 2010.

U.S. Department of Labor. 2009. Bureau of Labor Statistics. Available online at: http:// www.bls.gov/. Last accessed April 2010.

Western Wood Products Association [WWPA]. 1964-2010. Statistical yearbook of the western lumber industry. Portland, OR: Western Wood Products Association.

Wilson, A.K.; Spencer, J.S., Jr. 1967. Timber resources and industries in the Rocky Mountain States. Resour. Bull. INT-7. Ogden, UT: U.S. Department of Agriculture, Forest Service, Intermountain Forest and Range Experiment Station. 63 p.

USDA Forest Service Resour. Bull. RMRS-RB-12. 2012

45